Trailblazers

Twenty Amazing Western Women

by KAREN SURINA MULFORD

Foreword by SYBIL DOWNING

NORTHLAND PUBLISHING

For my sisters, Judy and Christine—
two of the strongest women I know.

The text type was set in Berkeley
The display type was set in Colwell, and Founders Caslon Twelve
Composed and Printed in the United States of America

www.northlandpub.com

FIRST IMPRESSION, 2001

01 02 03 04 05 06 07   7 6 5 4 3 2 1

ISBN 0-87358-783-9

Mulford, Karen.
Trailblazers : twenty great Western women / text by Karen Surina Mulford.
    p.   cm. — (The great American women series)
Includes bibliographical references and index.
ISBN 0-87358-783-9
1. Women pioneers—West (U.S.)—Biography. 2. West (U.S.)—Biography. 3. Frontier and pioneer life—
West (U.S.) I. Title. II. Series.

F596 .M75 2001
920.72—dc21   2001022217

Contents

FOREWORD *v*

INTRODUCTION *1*

SACAGAWEA
8

ESTHER HOBART SLACK MORRIS
16

BRIDGET BIDDY MASON
24

ABIGAIL SCOTT DUNIWAY
32

NELLIE CASHMAN
40

SARAH WINNEMUCCA
48

LOTTA CRABTREE
56

MARTHA HUGHES CANNON
64

MAY ARKWRIGHT HUTTON
72

MARY HUNTER AUSTIN
80

MARY JANE ELIZABETH COLTER
88

NELLIE TAYLOE ROSS
98

JEANNETTE PICKERING RANKIN
106

GEORGIA O'KEEFFE
114

MARY PICKFORD
122

DOROTHEA LANGE
130

JACQUELINE COCHRAN
138

MILDRED BABE DIDRIKSON ZAHARIAS
146

DOLORES FERNANDEZ HUERTA
154

SANDRA DAY O'CONNOR
162

BIBLIOGRAPHY *170*

INDEX *175*

FOREWORD

THE IMAGE OF THE WEST with its rugged individualism has largely shaped our national identity. Yet until recently, history texts as well as folklore created by dime novels and old movies led the world to believe that the West's only force was the white male. Women were mere stereotypes: the prostitute with a heart of gold, the gun-toting woman dressed in men's clothing, the long-suffering ranch wife, the Indian captive.

Then about twenty years ago, emerging scholarship revealed the actual story. From old letters and diaries, newspaper accounts and oral histories came evidence of women from all cultures and ethnic backgrounds, who had set back frontiers and made important contributions. In Trailblazers, Karen Surina Mulford reveals the fascinating lives of twenty such women.

As the title implies, the accomplishments of these women invariably broke new ground. Some orphaned as young children, some from comfortable back-grounds, the women all shared a determination to make something of their lives. Most chose to marry and have children, others did not. Either way, the road to their goal was never smooth. With true western "grit," each of these trailblazers refused to accept conventional boundaries and, instead, chose to follow her star. Reading about them is a delight and an inspiration.

—SYBIL DOWNING

INTRODUCTION

THE WESTERN FRONTIER, the region that so powerfully influenced the identity of the United States, has always belonged to women. A young Native American woman, with a baby strapped to her back, marked the frontier at its birth when she walked out upon the shores of the Pacific Ocean in 1805. Her name was Sacagawea, and she had just completed an arduous journey across uncharted territory with the Corps of Discovery, a trek that would be hailed "the greatest expedition ever undertaken in the history of this country."

This mysterious, unexplored land (that Lewis and Clark were sent to discover) had long been the homeland of various American Indian tribes. Sacagawea, born into the Shoshone tribe, had spent her childhood near the base of the Rocky Mountains—a land she would lead the explorers through on their historic journey. Although she was the teenage mother of a newborn son and the only woman on the expedition, Sacagawea contributed significantly to its success. As she trekked through dense forests, vast prairies, and treacherous mountain passes, she would also blaze trails through the West, lighting the way for other women to follow.

The twenty remarkable women featured in this book were all trailblazers in the American West. In their own ways, they were the movers and shakers in a new land where they found the inspiration, strength, and courage to follow their dreams, to challenge convention, and to create a better world for women.

The Western frontier would not appeal to women in the East until the 1840s, when hordes of men, women, and children packed up their belongings and set off for land that lay west of the Mississippi. Many came to find gold, others desired free land, and some wanted a fresh start in the West. They traveled on foot, horseback, or in covered wagons, and later arrived in stagecoaches, trains, automobiles, and airplanes.

For the pioneer women who crossed on foot, horseback, or covered wagons, the long westward journey involved incredible hardships. Many were forced to endure pregnancy, childbirth, disease, and death along the way, only to find at their destination, a raw, untamed land, so different from what they had left. But the weary women who survived the ordeal gained confidence and became stronger. They began casting off the old, confining roles that no longer seemed to

---

SACAGAWEA *by Frederick Coffay. Courtesy Western History Collection, Denver Public Library.*

apply in this virgin land, and began creating exciting new ones—often in areas that had been open only to men. With fresh skills and bold ideas, they became new women in a new land, determined and ready to shape the West into a better place.

All women who joined the westward migration did not come willingly. Biddy Mason, an African-American slave in Mississippi, had no choice in 1848 when her Mormon master decided to move his family and possessions to the Utah Territory. Biddy made the entire seven-month journey on foot, trailing behind her master's wagon, unaware that each step she took was bringing her closer to freedom and a self-made fortune in the West.

Five-year-old Martha Hughes Cannon also followed the Mormon trail to Utah, a rugged journey in a covered wagon that took the life of her sister and hastened her father's death. Martha became a physician, nursing school founder, and plural wife of a Mormon polygamist—the man she later defeated to become the first female state senator in Utah and in the country.

Rumors of abundant gold in California finally reached the East in the late 1840s, sparking the gold rush. Gold seekers by the thousands stopped whatever they were doing and fled to the goldfields of the West. Most left their families behind to fend for themselves, only to find when they reached the opposite end of the country, the days of easy pickings were over. The only way to make their fortunes involved backbreaking labor with a pick and shovel.

The few women who joined the gold rush would be transformed into some of the toughest women in American history. They learned to survive in rough, ramshackle mining camps that had been hastily built on some of the most rugged land on the frontier. These primitive camps were said to be no place for a woman, but these women came anyway, driven by the same gold fever that lured the men.

Pretty, petite Nellie Cashman caught the fever in San Francisco, listening to the tales her Irish friends told about lucky gold strikes. Before long, Nellie was out searching for the big bonanza, a quest that directed the rest of her life. A loner, Nellie prospected up and down the Western frontier, from the sun-baked deserts of Mexico to the frozen fields of Alaska. She would be called an angel, a saint, and a crazy prospector, but Nellie persevered and made several fortunes that she gave away to help the needy.

Battleship-sized May Arkwright Hutton also had dreams of finding gold in the West. She hopped aboard a train heading for Idaho in the late 1800s and found a land that suited her formidable size and personality. She used both to fight for the rights of miners and women, and to strike the big bonanza in the hard Idaho earth.

Most women who followed the gold rush to the West were not interested in pursuing a fortune by hurling a pick into the unyielding ground. These were entrepreneurial women who came to the gold camps to open bordellos, saloons, and boardinghouses. They found all the gold they needed in the pockets of lonely miners. Other women simply refused to be left behind when their gold-crazed husbands announced their plans to go West. They climbed up into the wagon beside their men, and accompanied them to the goldfields.

The majority of women, though, sent their husbands off and stayed home to tend the hearth. When they grew tired of waiting, they packed up the family and went to find their men somewhere out West. When Mary Ann Crabtree found her prospector husband, he was running a boardinghouse in a tiny California mining camp and still digging for gold. He could have saved himself the trouble. The family's fortune was not in the ground; it was lying at the feet of their talented daughter, who became the country's most celebrated and richest comedienne. By the time Lotta Crabtree was eight years old, she was charming the hearts and pockets of teary-eyed miners who showered the stage with more gold in one evening than Lotta's father had made in four years of prospecting.

As farmers, freeloaders, and prospectors charged across the Western frontier, invading the lands Native American tribes had occupied for centuries, conflicts erupted. The native tribes came to resent the wagonloads of white-skinned families who came to claim their homelands. The endless stream of settlers continued as war whoops and battle cries echoed across the frontier.

When the trouble reached the northern Nevada homeland of the Paiute, Sarah Winnemucca, the educated, articulate daughter of the Paiute's chief, persuaded her people to adopt an attitude of nonviolence when dealing with the white settlers. But when greedy government agents continued to inflict injustices on her people, Sarah organized a national campaign and took her cause across the country, delivering moving speeches and writing a book about the plight of the Paiute. She won the hearts of the public and an invitation to the White House to meet with the President.

The gun-toting, hard-drinking mining culture of the West did not provide the comforts many women may have enjoyed in the East. With the men off prospecting, these women were left to work the land, crack the whips, and handle a rifle. Since they were doing men's work, they wanted equal rights.

Women in the West were the first to win the right to vote and led the way to women's suffrage for their sisters across the land. It happened first in 1869 in the wild, reckless territory of Wyoming, where a year later, Esther Morris was named Justice of the Peace, the first woman in the country to hold the office. Wyoming would score another first in 1924 by electing Nellie

Tayloe Ross as governor, making her the first woman governor in the state and the nation.

In the Pacific Northwest, Abigail Scott Duniway would find fertile territory on which to sow the seeds for women's rights. An exceptional organizer, speaker, and publisher of a newspaper for women, Duniway would launch a crusade through Oregon and Washington and win suffrage for women.

In the Rocky Mountain state of Montana, another door opened for women when Jeannette Rankin became the nation's first Congresswoman in 1916. An outspoken pacifist and feminist, she would cause an uproar across the nation in 1917 when she voted against the country's involvement in World War I. The uproar would turn into a fury twenty-four years later when Rankin became the only member of Congress to vote against declaring war on Japan after the bombing of Pearl Harbor.

With the passage of the Nineteenth Amendment in 1920, all women were granted equal suffrage, so women in the West looked for new trails to blaze. Many women were swept off their feet at discovering a land so different from the one they had known and developed a burning passion to capture its essence in books, on canvas, or in structures.

The dry, haunting desert lands of the Southwest would inspire many artists and writers. When Mary Hunter Austin rode her horse onto the harsh desert landscape of southeastern California in the late 1800s, she was awestruck by a land so different from her farm home in the green hills of Illinois. She would come to love the stark desert where she found the inspiration to write eloquently of its wonders—creating novels and essays that would become literary classics.

Mary Jane Colter arrived in the Southwest in the early 1900s. Her fascination for the ruins of ancient cultures and the native art and crafts of the region inspired her long, remarkable career as architect and decorator for the Fred Harvey Company. Her recreated primitive structures still stand today, introducing Southwestern native arts to visitors around the world.

When artist Georgia O'Keeffe stepped off the train into the bright sunlight of New Mexico in 1929, she recognized immediately that her life had changed forever. So strong was the spell of the landscape, O'Keeffe returned every summer to capture on canvas her famous abstract impressions of the Southwest, the land where she would eventually move to and spend the remainder of her long life.

Above the spectacular desert terrain that attracted artists and writers were endless clear blue skies that drew an adventurous aviator named Jacqueline Cochran across the country. The skies above southern California provided a perfect training ground for Cochran to soar and practice the aerial maneuvers that enabled her to set numerous records in speed and sound. She would be

MARY PICKFORD *launched United Artists, a highly successful production and distribution company. Shown here with Douglas Fairbanks. Courtesy Mary Pickford Library.*

the first woman to break the sound barrier, and her achievements would open the skies to women.

Mary Pickford would also leave the East for more pleasant weather on the West Coast, which offered a climate more suitable for motion picture production. In southern California, Pickford would rise to stardom in a new industry that would sweep the nation. Curly-haired, sweet-faced Pickford was known as "America's Sweetheart" on stage and screen, but behind the scenes she was a shrewd negotiator who broke open the film industry to other performing artists by taking charge of her career and launching United Artists, a successful production and distribution company.

Well into the twentieth century, women in the West were charging into territories formerly held by men. Babe Didrikson Zaharias, an extraordinary athlete from Texas, would lead the way for women in competitive, professional sports. After she broke records and won Olympic medals in a variety of sports, "Babe" would spend the last part of her career as a champion woman golfer.

KATHARINE DREXEL, *a wealthy heiress from Pennsylvania, used her $20 million inheritance to establish schools and churches for Native Americans in the West. She became a nun and founder of a new order of Catholic sisters, and was canonized a saint in 2000 for miracles she was said to have caused. Courtesy Sisters of the Blessed Sacrament, Bensalem, Pennsylvania.*

After doors had been opened for women in politics, the arts, and sports, women in the West would champion the causes of others. Dolores Huerta's commitment to stop the exploitation of migrant farm workers led to the founding of the United Farm Workers Union. Dorothea Lange moved from New York to San Francisco to photograph wealthy socialites, but she turned her lens instead to Depression-era scenes in the streets and migrant farms, making poignant black-and-white photographs. After the bombing of Pearl Harbor, Lange photographed the indignities and injustices suffered by Japanese Americans during their forced relocation and internment, creating images so powerful they would be censored by the government.

Concern for justice would propel another Western woman through doors that had been previously closed to women, when, in 1981, Sandra Day O'Connor was appointed to the U.S. Supreme Court. When the former cowgirl from Arizona took her seat on the nation's highest court, she blazed yet another trail for women.

Along with the twenty women featured in this book are other women who influenced the history of the American West. Mitsuye Endo, a Japanese American woman from Sacramento, California, was twenty-two years old when she was ordered with her family to leave her home and go to an internment camp in Utah. A model citizen except for her heritage, Endo challenged the U.S. Constitution. The U.S. Supreme Court sided in her favor, bringing an end to this appalling episode in our country's history. Katharine Drexel, a wealthy heiress from Pennsylvania, used her $20 million inheritance to establish schools and churches for Native Americans in the West. She became a nun and founder of a new order of Catholic sisters, and she was canonized a saint in 2000 for miracles she was said to have caused. In the Pacific Northwest, in Vancouver, Washington, another nun, Mother Joseph, would contribute to the development of that pioneer community by building with her own hands a home for the sisters, an orphanage, a school, and a hospital, the first of many other organizations she would found during her lifetime.

The women you will read about in this book are as diverse as the Western landscape. Their stories will provide inspiration and portray a more complete image of women than the ones romanticized in the mythical Old West. The names of these twenty trailblazers are carved deeply into the Western terrain, where their spirits guide and encourage women everywhere.

SACAGAWEA

[ca. 1789–ca. 1812]

*The only female member
of the Lewis and Clark expedition is remembered for
her starring role in the discovery of
the American West, a journey she completed
with a baby strapped to her back.*

*T*HE SUDDEN SQUALL arrived in a fury. Raging winds plowed into the side of the boat, knocking it sideways. Another powerful gust tore the boom right from the hands of the startled crewman, leaving the sail to whip about wildly in the wind. The frightened helmsman let go of the tiller, and the boat heaved dangerously onto its side, spilling supplies into the foaming waters and endangering everyone in the boat, including a young Shoshone mother and her baby.

From the other side of the river, three hundred yards away, Captains Meriwether Lewis and William Clark watched the horrible scene unfold and agonized over the possible loss of lives and valuable supplies. Desperately trying to attract the crew's attention, they fired their rifles and shouted for the crew to cut the halyards and haul in the sail. But their shouts and shots were not heard.

There was no time to waste. The crew seemed to be in a panic, and the boat was quickly filling with water. Finally a muscular, experienced sailor realized the urgency and took command. He soon had the sails lowered and the boat righted, and when he shouted for buckets, the crew began bailing.

Throughout the terrifying ordeal, Sacagawea, the young Shoshone mother, remained calm and alert. She kept a watchful eye on her baby and on the important bundles belonging to Lewis and Clark that she had seen slipping into the river. While the rest of the crew bailed, Sacagawea leaned over the side and retrieved much of the valuable gear that had spilled overboard.

Statue of SACAGAWEA *on North Dakota State Capital Grounds, Bismarck, North Dakota. Courtesy State Historical Society of North Dakota.*

No woman has better claim to the title "Conquering Woman of the West" than Sacagawea, the only female member of the Lewis and Clark expedition, which journeyed across the American West in the early 1800s. This courageous young Shoshone woman, who is also called "Bird Woman," joined the expedition two months after giving birth and made the entire trip across the territory and back again with her infant son strapped to her back.

For nearly a century Sacagawea's name was not known throughout the country she served. Finally, in 1905, at a Lewis and Clark Exposition in Portland, Oregon, a statue of Sacagawea, with long braids, elkskin clothes, and a papoose on her back, was unveiled. Famous suffragette Abigail Scott Duniway praised the young Shoshone guide as "a symbol of all the unsung and unrewarded virtues of frontier womankind."

Once interest in Sacagawea was aroused, it seemed as if her name would endure forever, and in a variety of spellings. Books, films, and legends were created romanticizing her life, and Sacagawea's name can be found on monuments, mountains, lakes, and Girl Scout camps all across the country. More statues of Sacagawea exist than of any other woman in American history, yet there was never a photograph or portrait made of her.

Unlike others on the famous expedition, Sacagawea kept no journal, nor did she write letters or reports. With nothing to preserve Sacagawea's story in her own words, we can only know about her through the eyes and ears of the men who traveled with her across the West. In the pages of Lewis and Clark's journals, we learn about Sacagawea's intelligence, courage, and grace under pressure, and how important she was to the success of the expedition.

The exploration of the vast, mysterious area between the Mississippi River and the Pacific Ocean had been a persistent dream of Thomas Jefferson for many years. A few attempts had ultimately failed, and by the time Jefferson was sworn in as the third president of the United States in 1801, his dream of opening up the American West had become an obsession.

Jefferson chose his private secretary, Meriwether Lewis, and William Clark, a military man with frontier experience, to lead the historic expedition as an official United States Army unit, the Corps of Discovery. Their mission was to explore the land west of the Mississippi River, which had recently been purchased from France. By following the Missouri River to its source, the expedition was to find a passage through the mountains and float the Columbia River to the Pacific.

A corps of forty-two men launched the epic journey from St. Louis on May 14, 1804. Five months and fifteen hundred miles later, the party reached their first destination, the villages of the Hidatsa Indians in Dakota Territory.

George Catlin sketch of Mandan Villages. Courtesy Western History Collection, Denver Public Library.

The site, Fort Mandan, became the expedition's winter quarters, and the corps remained there until spring.

At the fort, Lewis and Clark met French Canadian fur trader Toussaint Charbonneau and his pregnant sixteen-year-old Shoshone wife, Sacagawea. When the explorers learned of Sacagawea's heritage, they determined that she could provide valuable assistance when they reached the source of the Missouri, the homeland of her people. Horses would be needed to cross the Rockies, and the Shoshone controlled the stock of horses in the area. Lewis and Clark hired Sacagawea and her husband to act as interpreters and guides.

The young woman selected to guide the expedition through the territory of her childhood was born about 1789 into the royal family of the Snake Indians (Shoshone) in what is Idaho today. Captured by the Minitaree tribe when she was about eleven years old, Sacagawea spent five years as a slave in the Mandan Indian villages before she was sold to Charbonneau.

A few months after Lewis and Clark hired the Charbonneaus, Sacagawea gave birth to a son named Jean Baptiste, later nicknamed "Pomp." Both captains, who were nearby during the birth, would note her tedious labor in their journals and mention a potion made from a rattlesnake's rattle that hastened the birth.

The Missouri River thawed a few months later in the spring, allowing the expedition to continue. On April 8, 1805, Lewis and Clark, thirty-one men, and Sacagawea, with the infant on her back, boarded six canoes and two pirogues and left Fort Mandan bound for the Pacific.

Throughout the journey, Lewis and Clark spent much time with the Charbonneau family, even sharing sleeping quarters with them. Perhaps this closeness was designed to prevent any embarrassing incidents between robust men and the only woman in the expedition. The idea must have been successful, as no mention of a problem appears in the journals of either Lewis or Clark.

The presence of the young Shoshone and her baby actually lifted the spirits of the men and relayed a signal of peace to the tribes they encountered on the journey. Sacagawea's baby son also became a source of pleasure for Clark, who later arranged to raise and educate "Pomp" as his own.

Trained from a very young age to forage food for her tribe, Sacagawea located edible plants that were used as a supplement to the expedition's diet and as sustenance when the food supply ran low. These skills earned the lone female in the party much respect and appreciation, especially from Lewis, who made numerous detailed notes about the various plants.

As impressed as the expedition party was by Sacagawea, her husband did not fare as well. When, during a violent storm, Charbonneau became frightened and refused to turn his boat into the wind, Lewis called the Frenchman "the most timid waterman in the world." His ineptitude caused the boat to nearly capsize, endangering everyone in the boat, including his wife and child. Fortunately, a strong crewman wrested the helm from Charbonneau and lowered the sails so the boat was able to right itself. Unlike her husband, Sacagawea kept a cool head throughout the ordeal, exhibiting maturity that impressed Lewis. "With her husband crying to his god for mercy," Lewis wrote, "Sacagawea calmly retrieved most of the precious cargo from the water." A week later the explorer honored Sacagawea by naming a picturesque stream Bird Woman's River.

As the Corps of Discovery neared the Great Falls of the Missouri River, Sacagawea was stricken with a high fever and became very ill. The expedition came to a halt as both captains applied various medical practices, including bleeding, to treat her condition. With her four-month-old baby son nearby, the weak young mother lingered painfully near death for six days, until a sulfur hot spring was located. Large quantities of sulfur water were administered and Sacagawea improved.

The Frenchman caused trouble again when Clark and the Charbonneau family were caught in a ravine during a rainstorm. When the rain turned into a torrential downpour, raging water thundered down the ravine, forcing the party to climb a steep bank to safety. With her husband in a state of shock and unable to assist his family, Sacagawea managed to climb to safety with her baby tucked under one arm, losing the baby's clothes, cradleboard, and bedding in the chaos.

As the expedition passed abandoned Indian camps, Sacagawea identified items and the camp's former inhabitants. When the boats reached a point on the Missouri River near a broad plain, she recognized the homeland of her people, the Lemhi Shoshone. Lewis recorded the incident in his journal. "The Indian woman recognizes the country and assures us that this is the river on which her relations live. This piece of information has cheered the spirits of the party, who now begin to console themselves with the anticipation of shortly seeing the head of the Missouri, yet unknown to the civilized world."

A few weeks later, Sacagawea pointed out another landmark, the summer retreat of her people, where the expedition would find the Shoshone. Although towering mountains blocked the view, Sacagawea assured the explorers that no impassable obstructions would imperil the journey. Lewis, who had never seen such gigantic mountains, was not convinced and believed the upcoming segment was "the most perilous and difficult part of our voyage."

The expedition needed horses in order to cross the Rockies, and the Shoshone controlled the area's horses. Sacagawea was the only one who could set the stage for friendly negotiations, for without horses the party would have to turn back.

The Shoshone acted standoffish and evasive, suspicious of the white men intruding on their homeland. But when Sacagawea later arrived at the meeting site, she was recognized and embraced by a childhood friend, an act that relaxed everyone present. More drama occurred later when Sacagawea was called to interpret during a meeting with the Shoshone Chief, Cameahwait. The chief was Sacagawea's brother, and when she first saw him, she ran to embrace him and wept profusely. Although the reunion was an emotional one for Sacagawea, she soon composed herself and resumed her duties as interpreter.

From this point on, negotiations proceeded smoothly as Sacagawea urged her people to trade with the white men and provide horses, guides, and items needed by the expedition to cross the mountains. When the trading was completed, the Corps of Discovery continued the journey across the Continental Divide on horseback. At this point, the Charbonneau family agreed to remain with the expedition until their return to Fort Mandan thirteen months later.

During the route through the Rockies, the expedition party wandered upon the homelands of many Indian tribes. But the sight of Sacagawea and her baby guaranteed a friendly welcome. During one pleasant stop, a Nez Percé chief told Clark that "no woman ever accompanies a war party of Indians in this quarter."

Heavy snowfall and icy trails made the trek through the mountains long and treacherous. When food rations ran out, the party was forced to eat horse meat.

By the time they arrived at the broad Columbia River on November 7, 1805, the party was weary and half-starved.

Construction began on winter quarters for the expedition party in a spruce forest near today's Astoria, Oregon. Sacagawea, agreeable and subservient throughout the journey, decided to assert herself when she heard that a whale had washed up on the beach several miles from camp. She insisted on being included on the two-day trek along the rocky coast. Her bold manner inspired Clark to note, "The Indian woman was very impatient to be permitted to go with me, and was therefore indulged. She observed that she had traveled a long way with us to see the great waters and that now that a monstrous fish was also to be seen, she thought it very hard that she could not be permitted to see either." Sacagawea was allowed to join the party, but when they reached the whale, only a skeleton remained, which Clark measured at 105 feet in length.

During the return trip to the Mandan villages, Sacagawea recommended certain routes that Clark followed, recording: "The Indian woman, who has been of great service to me as a pilot through this country, recommends a gap in the mountain more south, which I shall cross."

On August 17, 1806, the expedition reached the Mandan villages, where the Charbonneau family ended their journey. Charbonneau was paid a settlement of 500 dollars and 33 1/3 cents for his services, and Clark offered to take little nineteen-month-old Jean Baptiste back to Virginia with him to raise and educate. Sacagawea and her husband agreed but convinced Clark to wait until the boy was old enough to leave his mother.

A few years later, the Charbonneaus moved briefly to St. Louis, Missouri, where they entrusted their four-year-old son to Clark. True to his promise, Clark took custody of Jean Baptiste in 1809 and arranged for his education.

City life and homesickness eventually prompted Charbonneau and Sacagawea to move westward to Fort Manuel, a fur-trading post in the Dakotas. A fellow traveler on their return trip in 1811 wrote, "We had on board a Frenchman named Charbonneau with his wife, an Indian woman of the Snake (Shoshone) nation, both of whom had accompanied Lewis and Clark to the Pacific, and were of good service. The woman, a good creature, of mild and gentle disposition is greatly attached to the whites, whose manner and dress she tries to imitate, but she had become sickly and longed to revisit her native country."

Perhaps Sacagawea's reported illness was due to her pregnant condition. The following year, a clerk at Fort Manuel noted that on December 20, 1812, "the trapper's wife, a Snake Shoshone squaw, died of a putrid fever. She was good and the best woman in the fort, aged 25 years. She left a fine infant girl."

Reverend John Roberts and Andrew Basil at SACAGAWEA's *gravesite. Courtesy Western History Collection, Denver Public Library.*

Sacagawea's daughter, Lisette, was also raised by Captain William Clark.

Legends abound about Sacagawea living longer and dying in other places. However, in Clark's 1820 report on the status of Corps of Discovery members, he listed Sacagawea as already dead. Since he assumed responsibility for her children, Clark's words carry the most weight.

Although her life was brief, Sacagawea's contribution to the discovery of the American West lives on. She will be remembered forever as the Corps of Discovery's symbol of peace, a courageous young woman with a papoose on her back, who paved the way and guided a group of intruding "white men" across the rugged homeland of her people to the Pacific Ocean.

ESTHER HOBART
SLACK MORRIS

[1814–1902]

*She came to the wild Wyoming Territory
so her husband could search for gold, but Esther was the one
who made history by hosting a tea party that became
as important in the fight for women's rights
as the Boston Tea Party was in the American Revolution.*

LTHOUGH IT WAS HARDLY more than a shack, the humble miner's cabin had never looked better. Esther Morris had been up since dawn, cleaning and polishing, making sure everything would be sparkling and in place for the tea party. Twenty of the city's most influential citizens were coming, including the Democratic and Republican candidates for the legislature, two men who had no idea what their hostess had in mind for them.

Using her great charm, Esther mixed and mingled with her guests, seeing to their comfort and engaging them in interesting conversation. When she decided the time was right, she made her way across the room to where the two legislative candidates were standing. After offering more tea, Esther looked both men squarely in the eye and asked, "Will you introduce a bill in the new legislature that will give the women in Wyoming the right to vote?"

The fact that no woman in the world had such a right didn't matter to Esther Morris. She also knew, as did the two men standing in front of her, that women's suffrage was a subject of ridicule and condemnation by most men in the U.S. But Esther Morris was a fifty-five-year-old woman accustomed to fighting hard for what she wanted and winning. She quietly waited for a reply.

After a clearing of throats, the Democratic candidate answered first, promising that he would introduce a women suffrage bill if elected. The other candidate, not

ESTHER MORRIS *has been widely acclaimed as an influential figure in the events that established women's suffrage in Wyoming. Courtesy Wyoming Division of Cultural Resources.*

to be outdone, agreed to do the same if he was elected. What both men did not say was that they seriously doubted such a bill would ever reach a vote. But it wouldn't have mattered if they had said so, and it certainly wouldn't have discouraged the determined Esther Morris, who had successfully launched the first phase of her plan. The rest would be history.

When Esther Hobart Slack Morris arrived in the newly organized Wyoming Territory in the late 1860s, the gold rush was at its peak. She found a wild, wide-open land sprinkled with small communities of hard-drinking cowboys and rowdy miners with little to do but drink and fight. Gold seekers, gunslingers, and gamblers passing through on their way to California or Oregon outnumbered the permanent settlers. There were seven times more men than women, and of the three thousand people who lived there, most, like her husband, were hoping to make a fortune in gold.

Although the Wyoming Territory had just been organized, it was already known throughout the country as an untamed frontier with a high crime rate. But none of this bothered the formidable Esther Morris, who believed she had the solution to the Wild West problem. She was convinced that if women were granted full voting rights, the complexion of the population would change for the better. The right-to-vote privilege would act as a grand advertisement, attracting stable families to settle permanently in the Wyoming Territory. And what Esther Morris wanted, she usually managed to get.

Esther was a rare woman in her day, one who was not intimidated by confrontation and who had won many conflicts in her lifetime. Born in 1814 in Tioga County, New York, Esther Hobart Slack Morris was orphaned when she was eleven. She began taking care of herself soon after her parent's death, first as an apprentice to a seamstress, and later as a successful milliner and businesswoman. In 1842, when she was twenty-eight, Esther married John Slack, a civil engineer, with whom she had a son. When Slack died three years later, Esther moved to Illinois to settle her husband's estate, but was prevented from claiming title to a tract of land left to her because of discriminatory property laws. She was outraged at the legal difficulties faced by women and became committed to the women's rights movement and the words of activist Susan B. Anthony.

Esther later married a merchant, John Morris, with whom she had twin sons. In 1869 the family moved to a gold-rush camp in South Pass City, Wyoming Territory, where her husband opened a saloon and hoped to strike it rich in the goldfields of the West.

Esther Morris wasted no time getting a handle on things. On September 2, 1869, Wyoming was scheduled to hold its first territorial elections, an opportune time for Esther Morris to do something for women. She invited twenty of

In 1869 ESTHER MORRIS *and her family moved to a gold-rush camp in South Pass City, Wyoming Territory. Courtesy Wyoming Division of Cultural Resources.*

South Pass City's most influential citizens to her tidy miner's shack for tea. Among her guests were the two candidates for the legislature, Colonel William H. Bright, the Democratic candidate, and his Republican opponent, Captain Herman Nickerson.

During the evening, Esther approached each candidate, asking if he would introduce a bill in the new legislature that would grant the women of Wyoming the right to vote. No woman in the world had such a legal right, but that didn't prevent the determined Morris from pursuing the cause. Bright was aware of the sincerity of Morris's convictions, remembering that she had saved the life of his wife, Betty, by nursing her through a difficult childbirth. He respected Morris's intelligence, her abilities, and her skill as a nurse.

With women's suffrage often a subject for ridicule or condemnation by men in the U.S., both candidates probably doubted that such a bill would ever reach a vote. They each agreed to introduce a suffrage bill if elected.

William Bright won the election, and when it was over Morris took her campaign to the new legislator's wife. Betty Bright was an intelligent woman and a supporter of women's suffrage, who confronted her husband with the issue. Persuaded by his wife's arguments, the newly elected legislator made a strong statement before leaving for the legislature in Cheyenne: "I have made up my mind that I will do everything in my power to give you the ballot."

Bright kept his promises to his wife and Morris by drawing up a bill, "An Act to Grant to the Women of Wyoming Territory the Right of Suffrage and to Hold Office," which he introduced on November 9, 1869. The Wyoming territorial legislature assembled for the first time on October 1, 1869. Democrats made up the entire body, but a Republican with the power of veto held the office of governor. William Bright was named president of the Senate, a position of authority that gave him an opportunity to study the opinions of the men who made up the two houses of the legislature.

When he introduced his women's suffrage bill, Bright tried to convince his fellow legislators that the bill would show Republicans that Democrats were the more advanced party, adding that the bill would advertise Wyoming Territory as nothing else could. Most of his colleagues did not take the bill seriously and saw it as a way to embarrass the Republican governor, John Campbell, who would be faced with its veto. Few senators spoke out in opposition, and when the vote was taken, the results startled all Wyoming: six in favor, two opposed, and one absent. The bill was sent on to the House.

As the news about Bright's Female Suffrage Act spread throughout the Territory, Esther Morris saw golden opportunity. Along with other women, she wrote letters and made personal calls upon members of the legislature and the governor. The organized activity must have made an impact because Cheyenne's two newspapers heartily endorsed support of the bill after sensing the shift in public opinion. There were objections by some who felt that woman were unsuited to vote, and a few small newspapers printed comments about "giddy girls" taking control of Wyoming.

When the bill was finally introduced in the House, a powerful opposition group was prepared to kill it with amendments. One opponent suggested the age requirement be changed to thirty years instead of eighteen, convinced that women would never admit to being thirty and therefore wouldn't vote. The House passed only one amendment, the change in the voting age from eighteen to twenty-one. The fate of the Female Suffrage Act was now in the hands of Governor John Campbell, who was expected to veto the bill.

What the legislature did not know, however, was that Governor Campbell had once heard Susan B. Anthony speak and had been impressed by her arguments supporting women's rights. He signed the bill and thrust Wyoming Territory into the national spotlight as the first state or territory in the U.S. to grant full voting rights to its women.

Wyoming women were as amazed as the rest of the country at their new position as full citizens in a territory that had been organized barely a year before. One woman who may not have been surprised was Esther Morris, the

After she arrived in South Pass, ESTHER MORRIS *was appointed justice of the peace, the first woman to ever hold the office. Courtesy Wyoming Division of Cultural Resources.*

hostess who had set the miracle in motion when she asked some friends in for tea. Some would argue that The Esther Morris Tea Party had as much significance in the fight for women's rights as the Boston Tea Party had in the American struggle for independence.

One year later in 1870, South Pass was in need of a strong justice of the peace to keep order, and Morris's strong personality, large frame, and formidable air made her a perfect candidate for the job. Barely twelve months after she arrived in South Pass, Esther Morris was appointed justice of the peace, the first woman ever to hold the office.

Her position, as the first woman to hold judicial office in the world, attracted considerable publicity around the country. Some of the Eastern sporting papers printed cartoons of Esther Morris as being a formidable female who sat with her feet propped on the magistrate's desk, conducting her court with a cigar between her lips while whittling with a large jackknife, a heap of shavings nearby.

But South Pass City was satisfied with their stalwart Morris, who kept the peace and served out her term. Morris, happy in the role of peacekeeper, enjoyed serving her term and considered it a successful test "of a woman's ability to hold public office." Not one of the cases she tried was appealed, earning Morris the respect and admiration of the community for "administering justice with a vigorous and impartial hand."

Soon the women of wild Wyoming were in the news again, when the threat of lawlessness began brewing. After the completion of the Union Pacific Railroad, thousands of out-of-work railroad men filled the streets of Laramie. Men arrested for murder or cattle or horse stealing were found "not guilty" by the all-male juries who tried them. When the grand jury met in March 1870, women were named to jury duty.

A grand jury was appointed to hear a number of cases to consider the question of law enforcement. The fact that six men and six women sat on the jury together created another "first" in Wyoming that would make headlines throughout the world.

When news reached the East Coast that females sat on the grand jury in wild Wyoming Territory, newspaper reporters and artists were sent to cover this phenomenal event. When the women jurors refused to comply with requests for sketches, the artists used cartoon characters, as they had when Esther Morris was elected justice of the peace. Some newspapers poked fun at the women jurors, but inside the chambers the judge and citizens of Wyoming were dead serious. Women's suffrage had made an impact because women were called to serve as jurors as soon as their names appeared on lists of eligible voters. Before the next election they would make history again.

By the time women were finally able to exercise their right to vote, on September 6, 1870, the territory was well prepared for the onslaught of reporters who came to watch their women vote. Reporters had been coming to Wyoming often to report on its women. On this landmark Election Day, the press, politicians, and voting public were on their best behavior, prompting a chief justice to declare that the presence of women voters "has made our elections quite orderly."

In 1871 a group of disgruntled state Democrats, blaming women voters for the loss of several seats in the legislative elections, introduced a bill to repeal women's suffrage. One legislator stated, "I think women were made to obey. They generally promise to obey at any rate, and I think you had better abolish this female suffrage act or get up a new marriage ceremony to fit it." Another member of the house added that woman suffrage "will sap the foundations of society. Woman can't engage in politics without losin' her virtue." Although the act to repeal women's suffrage was passed by the legislature, Governor Campbell vetoed it.

Twenty years later, when Wyoming faced admittance to the Union, the "women issue" came up again. Many members of Congress opposed admitting a state where women had voting rights, advising Wyoming to take the vote away from women and enter as a state with only male voters. The Wyoming legislature refused and sent a telegram to Washington stating, "We may stay out of the Union a hundred years, but we will come in with our women."

Although the margin was narrow, Wyoming was admitted into the Union in 1889, the first state since New Jersey to include women's suffrage in its state constitution. It was an event that must have touched the heart and soul of Esther Morris, who had moved to Laramie after separating from her husband in 1871.

In 1873, Morris made a failed run for state representative, but continued to remain active in women's rights organizations and political affairs for the rest of her life. During Wyoming's statehood celebration in 1890, she was honored as a suffrage pioneer, and five years later at the age of eighty, she was elected a delegate to the national suffrage convention in Cleveland. Esther Morris died in Cheyenne in 1902.

The pioneering efforts of Esther Morris enabled women in Wyoming Territory to lead the rest of the country in the fight for women's rights. Her impact was also influential in the legislature's decisions to grant women property rights and to provide equal pay for male and female teachers. For her tireless devotion to women's rights, Esther Morris was honored with the title "Mother of Women's Suffrage," and in 1960, her statue was selected to represent Wyoming in Statuary Hall in the Capitol Building in Washington, D.C., and at the Wyoming state house in Cheyenne.

The rugged state that Esther Morris groomed continued to thrust its women into the national spotlight. After voting peacefully for several years, Wyoming women began tossing their hats in the political ring. They quickly set records by electing the first woman justice of the peace, the first woman state legislator, the first U.S. congresswoman, and the first woman governor. Quite an impressive history for a state known as "Wild Wyoming" when Esther Morris arrived.

BRIDGET BIDDY MASON

[1818–1891]

*Biddy Mason's journey from slavery
in the South to freedom and wealth in the West
happened one step at a time, like her trek
across the country, which she completed entirely on foot,
behind her master's wagons.*

OME ALONG, CHILDREN. There's no time to stop and play now. Help me bring that frisky lamb back before Master Robert finds out it's taken off again. Who knows what he'd do to us if it gets away," said Biddy to her two weary daughters. When the girls tore off in chase of the runaway lamb, Biddy sighed in relief, then bent her head and gently kissed the cheek of the baby sleeping in her arms.

Biddy's job on the strenuous two-thousand-mile westward journey was to mind the livestock, a seven-month-long task that Biddy and two of her three daughters, aged four and nine, completed entirely on foot. Holding her infant daughter in her arms, Biddy trudged behind her master's wagons across grassy prairies and parched deserts, in scorching sunlight and icy rains. She tended oxen, dairy cows, and mules, cooked meals, helped deliver babies along the journey, and cared for her own three children.

Biddy remembered how frightened she was a few months ago when she heard a rumor about Master Robert moving the Smith family and some of his slaves to the Utah Territory. Her eyes grew wide with terror as she thought about the possibility of being separated from her two daughters and the baby she was carrying. The master's word was law, and he had the power to do whatever he wished. As slaves, Biddy and her children were considered family possessions with absolutely no choice in the matter.

BRIDGET "BIDDY" MASON *amassed a fortune but never forgot her roots.*
Courtesy The Miriam Matthews Collection, California African-American Museum.

When the master came to the slave quarters to inform Biddy of his decision to take her and her children on the journey after her baby's birth, Biddy didn't know whether to laugh or cry. She had no desire to leave Mississippi, nor did she want to leave so soon after giving birth. But what could she do? Biddy was a powerless slave who loved her children, so she did as she was told. She gave birth to her third daughter in early January 1848, and was ready two months later when the Smith family's covered wagons began rolling westward as part of a caravan of three hundred wagons.

Biddy Mason was born into slavery in the early 1800s, a time when African Americans had no legal rights and very few opportunities. Those individuals who visited the West were undoubtedly free white men who returned to their homes in the East with reports of great opportunities and freedom. Their words inspired thousands of families to pack up their belongings and go West in the only fashion available at the time, in covered wagons pulled by oxen. Among the families who made the long westward trek were Southerners, who brought along wagonloads of household possessions, including their slaves.

By the time Biddy arrived in California in 1851, slavery had been outlawed in the state for more than a year. Without a penny to her name, this patient, hardworking woman found a way to freedom, employment, and wealth in the West. She became a landowner, entrepreneur, philanthropist, and inspiration to those who shared her belief in the American dream.

Biddy was born in Hancock County, Georgia, in 1818. Although she was named Bridget at birth, she was called "Biddy," a name she would carry the rest of her life. Like other slaves, Biddy was not sent to school and never learned to read or write. She was trained instead in the more practical arts of animal husbandry, nursing, and midwifery.

When she was eighteen, Biddy and her sister were sold to Robert Marion Smith, a wealthy plantation owner from Mississippi who needed slaves to care for his frail wife and six children. Biddy arrived in Mississippi during a time when the first Mormon missionaries were carrying their message to wealthy plantation owners in Alabama, Mississippi, and North Carolina. Ten years later, in 1847, Robert Smith and his wife were converted to Mormonism and decided to follow the Mormon migration to the Utah Territory. He assembled his family and all his personal property, which included Biddy and her three daughters, reputedly fathered by Smith.

Biddy was thirty-two years old when the Smith family's wagons began rolling to the West. Her responsibility was to herd the livestock and, like her charges, Biddy and her daughters completed the strenuous seven-month journey to Salt

Lake City on foot, trudging across the country behind her master's wagons.

The Smith family remained in Utah for only a few years. In 1851 Robert Smith was ready to move his family and slaves to San Bernardino, California, where a new community of Mormons was being established. Biddy was assigned the same task she performed on the earlier trek across country, to herd the family's livestock. This time she was unaware that each step she took on her walk to California would bring her closer to freedom.

In 1850, a year before the Smith family's arrival in San Bernardino, California had been admitted to the Union as a free state. If Smith knew of slavery's illegal status either before or after his arrival in California, he preferred to ignore it.

For a slave, California was indeed a golden state, offering freedom, an independent lifestyle, and the possibility of striking it rich in the goldfields. Although Biddy and her family met free blacks in San Bernardino, Biddy and her teenage daughters remained slaves in the Smith household for three more years. In 1854, when Smith decided to move his family and possessions to Texas, Biddy was horrified. She was aware that Texas was a slave state, and she feared that if she moved there with her daughters, they might never be free. When the distraught Biddy revealed her fears to two free young black men who were romantically involved with her daughters, the men promised to find help from others who were also committed to antislavery causes.

The local sheriff's office understood Biddy's dilemma and provided valuable assistance by drawing up a writ to prevent Smith from taking Biddy and her family out of the state of California against their wishes. When Smith discovered that local authorities might intercept his escape route to Texas, he set up a camp for his family in the Santa Monica Mountains of Los Angeles. When a group of free black supporters and the sheriffs of Los Angeles and San Bernardino counties discovered the hideout, they placed the Mason family in protective custody. Biddy served Smith with an order to appear in court.

Although California was a free state at the time, it still had laws like the Civil Practice Act of 1850, which stated that no person of color could testify in court against a white person. Biddy Mason was forced to worry and wait outside the courtroom on the first day of the trial in Santa Monica in 1856, unable to hear Smith lie to the judge about the desire of his slaves to move willingly to Texas with him.

When the judge questioned Mason in his chambers about the move to Texas, she related her fears and wishes to stay in California. On the following day, January 21, 1856, Smith failed to appear in court. Mason petitioned the court and won her freedom as well as the freedom of her daughters and the remainder of Smith's slaves. As he granted their freedom, the judge informed the petitioners "to become settled and go to work for themselves—in peace and without fear."

Biddy Mason's two-day trial became a landmark civil rights case and an important test of the California constitution. Had this case come to trial a year later, Mason probably would not have gained her freedom. In the Dred Scott decision of 1857, the United States Supreme Court ruled that slaves moved from a slave state to a free state did not become free and were not entitled to the rights of a federal citizen. It would be several more years before the Civil War ended and slavery was finally abolished with the passing of the Thirteenth Amendment to the Constitution in 1865.

Now that she was free, Biddy selected the surname Mason and moved with her daughters to Los Angeles into the home of the Owens family. A lifetime bond would develop between these two families and lead to a marriage between one of Biddy's daughters and Charles Owens.

Mason's skills as a midwife and nurse enabled her to find employment as a practical nurse for a prominent Los Angeles doctor. She yearned for a home of her own and lived frugally for ten years, saving enough money to buy two lots on ten acres of land on the edges of the city in 1866. She called the site located at 331 South Spring Street, "the homestead," and cautioned her children never to abandon it. She built a two-story brick house with two storerooms on the lower floor and living quarters on the upper level. Later Mason had rental units constructed on the property, which she leased to commercial operations. By maintaining her frugal lifestyle, Mason was able to purchase other parcels in the area, which she later sold for a profit.

In 1872 Mason hosted a meeting at her home for several of her friends in the community. The meeting resulted in the founding and financing of the city's first black church, the Los Angeles branch of the First African Methodist Episcopal Church. Mason donated the land on which the church would be built and paid the annual taxes and the minister's salary.

Mason had been saving money for eighteen years, earmarked for the building of a structure that would produce revenue. For years she had watched as other newcomers in Los Angeles purchased land and became successful, and she had witnessed this city's change from a dusty cattle town into a booming commercial center with fifty thousand residents. Mason was convinced that nineteenth-century Los Angeles would one day develop into an even bigger, important urban center.

BRIDGET BIDDY MASON's *"homestead" at 331 South Spring Street in Los Angeles, California. Courtesy The Miriam Matthews Collection, California African-American Museum.*

In 1884, when Mason was sixty-six, she sold a portion of the original "homestead" property for $1,500 and began construction on a large commercial building with rental spaces on the remaining land. The site of Mason's purchase, which once sat on the fringes of Los Angeles, became a busy commercial operation in the heart of the city. By 1890 Spring Street between Fourth and Seventh had become the financial center of Los Angeles, a city of over 50,000, including 1,258 blacks. Today Biddy's $250 original purchase is now a $24-million high-rise shopping center and parking garage called the Broadway Spring Center.

Mason patiently and wisely continued investing in real estate, and her finances grew along with the city she believed in and claimed a stake in. Mason amassed a fortune of almost $300,000, and her land holdings in Los Angeles provided her family with a source of wealth and status in the community. Her grandson, Robert Curry Owens, who with his brother started a livery stable on the homestead, became a real estate developer, politician, and, at one time, the richest African American in Los Angeles.

MASON *founded the city's first black church, the Los Angeles branch of the First African Methodist Episcopal Church. Courtesy The Miriam Matthews Collection, California African-American Museum.*

As Mason built her fortune, she never lost sight of her roots. She remained sensitive to the needs of others throughout her life, and in her later years, turned her homestead into a base for numerous charitable operations. As lines formed at her door, Mason responded with donations of land for schools, churches, and hospitals; aid for flood victims; and time, money, and food for the needy. Stranded travelers were provided refuge in her home, and Mason often visited prisoners in the jails, where she hoped to relieve their loneliness. Along with her daughter Ann, Mason operated fourteen nursing homes and deeded some property to her grandsons.

Biddy Mason died at seventy-three, on January 15, 1891, with a line of people waiting outside her door to see her. While the city mourned, she was buried at Evergreen Cemetery in an unmarked grave in the Boyle Heights neighborhood of Los Angeles. In her obituary, the Los Angeles *Times* wrote that Mason was "a pioneer humanitarian who dedicated herself to forty years of good works."

The legacy of Biddy Mason, the slave who walked her way to freedom, lived on in the memories of all who knew her. In 1988, nearly a century after her death, a handsome new tombstone was placed on her grave during a ceremony attended by Mayor Tom Bradley and thousands of members of the First African Methodist Episcopal church. A year later, Mason was honored once again when a memorial in her name was unveiled at the Broadway Spring Center in Los Angeles on November 16, 1989, a day that had been declared "Biddy Mason Day."

ABIGAIL SCOTT DUNIWAY

[1834–1915]

*Women who are not ready
to go down into the very cesspool of politics,
and so trouble the waters there that the angel of Freedom
may have opportunity to enter and purify it,
do not deserve the blessing of individual liberty. . . .*

—Abigail Scott Duniway

*S*EVENTEEN-YEAR-OLD Abigail Scott could feel her heart pounding with excitement as she watched her father struggle to maneuver the heavy wagon into place behind a caravan of covered wagons that stretched ahead in an endless line. The day Abigail had been dreaming about for the past year had finally arrived. It was April 2, 1852, the day the Scott family would begin their journey to Oregon, the "Eden of the West."

Another reason for Abigail's happy state of mind was the assignment her father had given her, to record the six-month overland trip in her journal. She had already begun the task, noting the items that the family had agreed to pack in the five wagons they would haul across the country on the long westward trek. She could hardly wait to record the adventures that lay ahead.

The teenager's high spirits were suddenly dampened by the sound of weeping coming from the back of the wagon. Abigail recognized the sobs and knew they belonged to her mother, who was still weak from the birth of her last child, her twelfth. For the first time since her father decided to make the journey, Abigail was struck with fear for the frail, unhappy woman who had prayed and

---

ABIGAIL SCOTT DUNIWAY *established* THE NEW NORTHWEST, *a newspaper for women in 1871 bearing the motto "Free Speech, Free Press, Free People." Courtesy Oregon Historical Society.*

pleaded to be left behind in Illinois. Could her mother survive the long journey across prairies and canyons, rivers and mountains, through good weather and bad? Abigail also wondered why men made the decisions and women were stuck with the results.

The worried teenager had no way of knowing in 1852, as she traveled the rugged Oregon Trail in the largest mass migration in American history, that she would one day be honored as one of the nineteenth century's greatest suffragists and earn a distinguished place in history. But first Abigail Scott would have to champion the cause of suffrage across the Pacific Northwest, where she would find the road to women's rights as difficult as her journey through the Rockies in a covered wagon.

Abigail Scott was born in 1834 in a log cabin in Groveland, Illinois, to a sobbing mother and a father raging because she wasn't a boy. As in many frontier families, sons were preferred for their strength and assistance with farming chores and heavy field labor. The rejection Abigail felt for not having been born male continued to haunt her throughout her life and help mold her into a defensive, belligerent child who despised domesticity as much as her family's Calvinist notions of salvation and damnation.

Her memories would include a harsh childhood with ten siblings and an endless cycle of never-ending chores dominated by an insensitive, authoritarian father. She remembered her mother as a frail, weary woman who complained often about the hard life of a woman. Even though Abigail matured into a witty, outspoken young woman, the memory of her mother's pitiful life and lack of authority would fill her with anger and disgust for the status of women.

Abigail's father found it hard to resist the lure of the West after the passage of the Oregon Donation Land Act of 1850. The act entitled every man to 320 acres of land and another 320 if he had a wife. Ignoring the protests of his sickly wife, Abigail's father made the decision two years later to add his family's wagons to the long caravan of covered wagons bound for the Eden of the West.

Abigail excelled at her responsibility of recording the six-month overland trip in her journal. The adventure gave her a host of subjects to write about, including storms, diseases, and deaths of her mother, youngest brother, and cousin. Her journal would also fuel the books and poetry she wrote later in her life.

Once the Scott family had settled in Oregon, Abigail taught school briefly before she "met her fate," the handsome, kindhearted Benjamin Duniway. In 1853 the intelligent, spirited eighteen-year-old schoolmarm married the tall, gentle farmer and rancher, repeating wedding vows that excluded the word "obey."

Ben moved his bride to a farm on a lonely, wild stretch of land, where Abigail became pregnant immediately with her first child and only daughter,

Clara. Three years later, after a difficult labor, a son would be born. Soon Abigail found herself living the life of her mother, saddled with young children and endless rounds of farm chores. She found consolation in writing poetry, the publication of which in the local newspaper became a springboard to a writing career for this imaginative woman.

Several years later, in 1859, the Duniway family moved to Yarnhill County. Abigail wrote a novel based on her Oregon Trail journal entitled *Captain Gray's Company*, which became the first commercially printed novel in Oregon. She also wrote columns for the *New Oregon Farmer* and bore two more children.

The family was forced to move yet again when they lost their land after a friend defaulted on bank notes that Ben had cosigned. Appalled that she could do nothing about it, the indignant Abigail huffed, "I was my husband's silent partner— a legal nonentity with no voice or power for self protection under the sun."

The Duniways moved to Lafayette and bought a small home, which Abigail turned into a school. Things went along well for a few years until Ben was injured in an accident and left a semi-invalid. To support her family, which had grown to include six children, Abigail opened a millinery shop and worked hard to turn it into a financially successful venture. After the difficult birth of her last child, her fifth son, Abigail decided to take control of her own body through abstinence, a decision that was supported by her understanding husband.

The millinery shop also became a haven for desperate women, who gathered regularly to share their accounts of the injustices they suffered from not having any ownership rights. Abigail began writing about her clients and their abuses, and became increasingly aware of the inequalities that existed between men and women. When she shared her stories with her husband, she complained that "one half of the women are dolls, the rest of them drudges, and we're all fools." The understanding Ben convinced his outraged wife that nothing would change until women were able to vote. Remembering how her mother lost her life on a journey she never wanted to make, Duniway decided to create a better world for women, an ambitious decision that became a guide for the rest of her life.

By 1870 Abigail was ready to do something about the status of women. She organized the Equal Rights Society of Oregon and moved her family to Portland, near her brother Harvey. She had long been envious of her brother, the Scott family favorite and current editor of the influential *Portland Oregonian*. When Harvey refused to print some of his sister's articles about women's rights, Abigail established a newspaper for women by herself. A year later, in 1871, she launched *The New Northwest* bearing the motto "Free Speech, Free Press, Free People."

With her two sons running the presses, Abigail wrote editorial copy and advice columns and promoted the entire agenda of women's issues, including

ABIGAIL SCOTT DUNIWAY *at the polls, 1914. Courtesy Oregon Historical Society.*

suffrage. She targeted her lively weekly for readers throughout the Pacific Northwest and drew supporters from all over the frontier. Isolated farmers' wives, eager to read about their sisters in the East, were among the paper's biggest fans and continued to support the paper through its sixteen-year run.

Once she had the paper up and running, Duniway was ready to take her campaign for women's rights across the Northwest. She persuaded Susan B. Anthony, the biggest name in women's suffrage at the time, to come to the Northwest and accompany her on a two-month tour through Oregon and Washington. Traveling by steamboat, wagon, horseback, and canoe, the two suffragists spread their message to women in the backcountry, churches, and city halls. When they were pelted with rotten eggs and accused of being alcoholics and immoral women, Duniway became all the more determined in her fight for women's rights.

Duniway's quick wit often saved her when she was faced with male opposition. At one of her lectures, when a man argued against suffrage by remarking, "I have often known a hen to try to crow, but I've never seen one yet," Duniway promptly replied, "I once saw a rooster try to set, and he made a failure too."

For the next sixteen years, Duniway traveled for six months out of each year throughout her newspaper's scope, the Northwest Territory—Oregon, southern Idaho, Washington, Puget Sound, and coastline areas. For the lonely frontier women, Abigail brought dreams of a new world for themselves and their off-spring. While she traveled, Abigail kept an ongoing narrative about the people she met and published the pieces in *The New Northwest*. She managed to write several books, including her autobiography and an epic poem, and lectured in any available town halls or village squares, churches, or back rooms of taverns. Throughout her campaign, Duniway had the comfort of knowing that her family back in Oregon was well cared for by Ben and her daughter, Clara.

In 1869, when Wyoming and Utah became the first states to grant women suffrage, the issue was fervently contested in other Western states. Soon women all over the nation were taking notice, inspiring Duniway to cross the country four times during the next twenty years to attend National Woman Suffrage Association conventions in the East. She used whatever transportation was available, be it steamship or stagecoach, to take her message to legislators and women's groups, impressing them with her indomitable spirit and Western ambition. When she spoke to a packed audience at the Philadelphia Centennial Exposition in 1876, she was applauded for her independent frontier ways.

The success of her newspaper and the notoriety from her lecture tours gave Duniway the necessary clout to gain approval from the Oregon state legislature for the Sole Trader Bill. This bill allowed a woman engaged in business to regis-ter the fact with the county clerk, thereby protecting her tools, furniture, and stock from seizure by her husband's creditors. If a husband abandoned his wife, she could obtain the court's permission to sell or lease property, make contracts, and collect money due him.

As Duniway continued her relentless campaign for women's rights, suffrage bills were introduced in Washington, Idaho, and Oregon. In 1884, when she was elected vice president of the National Woman Suffrage Association, Duniway was considered the representative of frontier women.

In 1886, when the temperance movement became an issue in Oregon, Duniway initially thought it would provide an opportunity for her to reach more people. But she soon came to the conclusion that the temperance issue would not benefit the suffrage movement. She believed that most men would not sup-port prohibition because it would take away their freedom.

Not wanting to alienate males from supporting the suffrage cause, Duniway voiced her opposition to the Prohibition Party and wrote editorials claiming that alcoholism was a physical problem, not a moral evil. When word spread of her disagreement over linking the women's right to vote with prohibition of alcohol, Duniway was accused of "selling out to whiskey" by her sisters in the East.

Undaunted, Duniway continued her fight to keep the suffrage issue separate from prohibition by maintaining that "prohibition was not temperance, but intolerance and quackery." When word reached the Woman's Christian Temperance Union in the East, they were outraged by her charges and retorted that Duniway was a disgrace to the suffrage cause. Ignoring the accusations, Duniway continued to follow the advice she so freely dispensed, "Do not yield to difficulties, but rise above discouragements."

As if the opposition of prohibitionists in 1886 wasn't enough for Abigail Duniway to contend with, she would also face the loss of her only daughter, Clara, to tuberculosis. It was also a time of family unrest, her sons growing tired of the newspaper and eager to pursue their dream of becoming ranchers on land available through the Preemption Act, Homestead Act, and Desert Reclamation Act.

The idea of ranching also appealed to Duniway, who harbored notions of establishing a cooperative women's community. She sold her newspaper with the understanding that she would continue writing for it to promote women's issues. When the new owner went out of business two months later, Duniway's public platform for suffrage disappeared with it. The proceeds from the sale of the paper did enable the Duniway men to purchase a ranch in Idaho, but Abigail chose to spend most of her time in Portland, where Ben would return to spend the final years before his death in 1896.

When the suffrage bill lost in Oregon in 1884, 1900, 1906, and 1908, Abigail kept on working for its passage, even though rheumatoid arthritis had confined her to a wheelchair. Her persistence would prove instrumental in winning suffrage in Idaho in 1896, in Washington in 1910, and finally in Oregon in 1912. It would take five referendums before Duniway's home state would pass the suffrage bill, a frustrating situation which her prohibitionist sisters in the East blamed on Duniway's earlier opposition.

After Abigail tossed her hat in the ring and began her crusade for women's rights, fifty years passed before the Nineteenth Amendment gave all American women the right to vote. But for Abigail Scott Duniway, the issue was always more than winning the suffrage issue. Her long campaign trail is littered with arguments against injustices to women and battles for married women's property rights, which Oregon legislators granted in 1878.

A woman ahead of her time, Duniway also championed the cause of a married woman's right to control her body by limiting her pregnancies, an issue that appalled many but earned support among the frontier and farm women of the Pacific Northwest. Duniway stayed involved in women's affairs to the end, serving as president of the Oregon State Women's Suffrage Association and the State Federation of Women's Clubs. When Duniway was seventy-eight years old,

ABIGAIL SCOTT DUNIWAY *was the first woman to register to vote after the suffrage amendment was adopted. With county clerk J. B. Coffey. Courtesy Oregon Historical Society.*

her home state awarded her the ultimate honor of signing the official Suffrage Proclamation after it became law in 1912. Two years later, in 1914, she was the first woman to cast a vote in Oregon. She died the following year at the age of eighty-one.

For fifty years Abigail Scott Duniway fanned the flames of women's suffrage across the Pacific Northwest and established a solid foundation for women's equality across the country. Her legacy continued long after her death, keeping the fire of women's rights burning for generations to follow.

NELLIE CASHMAN

[1845–1925]

It gives me a great deal of pride
to go back to every place I've ever been and
look folks square in the eye
and know I've paid my bills and played the game like a man.

—Nellie Cashman

HEN THE MOON was high enough, Nellie calmly climbed up into her buggy, gently flapped the reins, and urged the horses into a slow, easy pace. She led them as quietly as possible through the dark, deserted streets of town to a house on a hilltop south of the city, where she pulled to a stop.

A man emerged from the shadows and quickly climbed up beside Nellie. Hardly making a sound, he slid his large frame onto the floor of the buggy out of sight. In a leisurely manner, Nellie directed the horses back through the streets of Tombstone to a point well beyond the city limits. Then, letting out a shout, she whipped her team into a gallop and rumbled off into the night, bound for the depot at Benson, where her grateful passenger would board a waiting train.

Nellie Cashman had just saved the life of E. B. Gage, superintendent of the Grand Central Mining Company, who was to be kidnapped and lynched that very night by an angry group of miners. Indignant Nellie had used her courage and ingenuity to outsmart a group of men once again, a familiar situation for this tough little woman who dedicated most of her life to the pursuit of the elusive mother lode.

The promise of abundant gold and silver finds drew hundreds of thousands of people to the American West during the territorial years. A lucky claim could land a man more money in an instant that he could earn in a lifetime. The mere rumor of a strike could create an instant community of men armed with picks,

NELLIE CASHMAN *was an ambitious prospector and shrewd business-*
woman. Courtesy Arizona Historical Society.

shovels, and dreams of making millions in the mining districts of California, Nevada, and Arizona, or as far north as Canada and the Yukon.

As a rule, the women who ventured westward did not share the same prospecting vision. The more adventurous dreamed of getting rich in brothels, boardinghouses, and gambling houses, cashing in on the fortunes of the lonely miners. One exception to this rule was a petite Irish lass named Nellie Cashman, who chased her dream of hitting the big bonanza up and down the Western frontier.

Barely five feet tall and weighing less than a hundred pounds, the courageous and spirited Nellie was hardly the typical nineteenth-century woman. Unbound by convention, she played by her own rules, blazing trails through the dry desert of the American Southwest to the frozen wilderness of the Yukon. Although the prospecting life that Nellie chose was a rough and lawless one, filled with gun-toting, hard-drinking men, Nellie would earn the respect and admiration of her fellow miners.

Nellie was an ambitious prospector and shrewd businesswoman, but she also had a soft spot in her heart for the needy. A devout Catholic, she firmly believed charity was her duty and built a reputation for her compassionate nature and good deeds. Once during an interview she explained, "After all, we pass this way only once, and it's up to us to help our fellows when they need our help."

Nellie practiced what she preached, giving generously to causes that improved the lives of those in need. She founded hospitals and churches, fed the hungry, grubstaked down-and-out miners, and braved impossible elements to rescue her fellow miners. Those who knew Nellie considered her a heroine, a savior, and an angel of the frontier. They also acknowledged that Nellie was an independent and driven hardheaded miner infected with a bad case of gold fever.

Ellen "Nellie" Cashman was born in Queenstown, Ireland, in the County Cork in 1845 during the disastrous Great Potato Famine. When she was five years old, Nellie migrated to the United States with her widowed mother and younger sister, and settled in Boston, Massachusetts. By the late 1860s, the family was on the move again, this time across the country to the West Coast, where in San Francisco, California, the Irish made up one-third of the population.

Here in the city by the bay, Nellie listened to her countrymen tell tales of lucky miners striking it rich in the mountains, valleys, and deserts of the West. Before long, Nellie was also consumed by prospecting fever, a condition that would direct the rest of her life and drive her to more than twenty mining camps and towns before she died.

Nellie's first mining venture came in 1872, when she moved with her mother to the wild silver-mining district of Pioche, Nevada. After prospecting in the

NELLIE CASHMAN *standing in front of a store in Yukon. Courtesy Arizona Historical Society.*

surrounding hills, Nellie knew she could never get by on the unsteady income of a miner and promptly opened a boardinghouse. After a few years in Pioche, the two Cashman women went back to San Francisco, where Nellie left her mother in the care of her sister and joined the gold rush north to Canada.

In the company of two hundred miners from Nevada, pint-sized Nellie trekked north to Cassiar in the extreme northwest corner of British Columbia, a few miles from Yukon Territory. As she had in Nevada, Nellie opened a board-inghouse for miners. She also began mining gold-placer ground and learned the basic elements of mining geology. Her charitable heart soon had Nellie tapping her customers for donations to help build a hospital for her dear friends, the Sisters of St. Anne, in nearby Victoria, British Columbia.

It was while she was visiting with the good Sisters in Victoria during the winter of 1874–75 that Nellie was elevated to the status of heroine. Word was sent to Nellie that her fellow Cassiar miners were trapped in a severe winter storm and suffering from scurvy. Wasting no time, Nellie gathered supplies and sleds, then hired six men and sailed to Alaska. Once they reached land, the small party proceeded to trek inland through dangerous heavy snows, against the wishes of the local army commandant. Fearing the worse, he ordered his soldiers to rescue the party.

When the soldiers finally found Nellie, she was encamped on the ice of the Stickeen River, humming a lively tune and cooking over a wood fire. Nellie and her party had struggled through seventy-seven days of bitter mountain weather before reaching the trapped miners. After the rescue, the young woman with the Irish brogue became the talk of the West, known as "The Angel of the Cassiars."

Industrious, ambitious, and pretty as a Victorian cameo, Nellie was also a savvy entrepreneur. Running businesses and prospecting were two occupations that Nellie combined throughout the remainder of her life. A shrewd "stampeder," Nellie liked to arrive at a mining camp during the early stages, make a profit, and then move on. It was the sense of adventure that excited Nellie most, evidenced by the fact that she made several fortunes throughout her lifetime but gave most of her money to charity.

The years spent in the Northland had provided Nellie with plenty of hands-on mining experience, and in 1879, when she heard about strikes in California and Arizona, she was anxious to try her luck. Stops in Los Angeles and Yuma, Arizona, proved disappointing, so Nellie continued on to Tucson and opened a restaurant. A few months later, though, she heard about a great silver strike in Tombstone, eighty miles away. So off she went to try her luck in "the town too tough to die," where she spent the most-documented years of her life.

Nellie opened a boot and shoe shop in Tombstone and later a grocery and hotel and dining room, called the Russ House. Nellie could wield a spatula as expertly as a pick and shovel, and she soon had the community eating out of her hands. The Russ House on Toughnut Street became as famous as the nearby Bird Cage Saloon and OK Corral, with a clientele that included Doc Holliday, Johnny Ringo, and Wyatt Earp.

Nellie lived in Tombstone from 1880 to 1887, buying and selling claims and amassing a fortune. She also won the admiration of the town for helping establish the town's first hospital and first Roman Catholic Church. Nellie often fed and housed free of charge those unable to pay, and solicited assistance from everyone she knew, including madams of the red light district, prisoners in jail, and mining magnates, all equal contributors in Nellie's eyes.

During her years in Tombstone, Nellie's widowed sister, Fanny, became ill with tuberculosis in San Francisco. After traveling to San Francisco, Nellie decided to move her sister and her five children to Tombstone, where she could care for them. After Fanny died a few years later, "Aunt Nell" became the sole support of her nieces and nephews.

Wherever she lived, Nellie was regarded with respect, a situation that made it fairly easy for Nellie to enlist the aid of others. Her close relationships with Roman Catholic priests and sisters at boarding schools in Arizona and California allowed Nellie to provide her nieces and nephews with first-rate educations.

In 1883, when word about a gold strike in Baja California reached Tombstone, Nellie organized a twenty-one-man prospecting party. She then led the group to Mexico, across the Gulf of California, and inland to the deserts of Baja. Failing to find the gold, the party nearly perished in the intense heat without water. But the story goes that Nellie left the party to search for help and returned a few days later with water and a rescue party.

Then there was the time in 1884, when Nellie heard about a plan by local authorities to turn the hanging of five convicted robbers into a spectacle. Furious, Nellie climbed onto her soapbox and railed against the greedy promoters. She also recruited a group of sympathetic miners to destroy a newly erected grandstand for the "necktie party."

Nellie was up in arms again a few months later when she heard of the intended lynching of a local mining official. Incensed, Nellie drove to the official's home, hid him in the back of her buggy, and whisked him away to the railroad station, where he escaped safely.

When mining had finally played out in Tombstone in 1887, Nellie became restless to move on to new territory. When she heard about a lucky strike in Kingston, New Mexico, she was off, hoping for the big bonanza. She left soon afterward for the rich gold-quartz deposits in the Harquahala Mountains of western Arizona. Nellie prospected the region thoroughly and actually owned one of the better claims there. There was talk of Nellie almost marrying one of Harquahala's original discoverers, but the rumor was false. Nellie openly admitted that she enjoyed the company of men over women, but she never married, keeping her private life to herself and claiming that she "hadn't had time for marriage." She also told an *Arizona Daily Star* reporter that she preferred "being pals with men to being cook for one man."

After leaving Harquahala, Nellie spent the next several years trying her luck at various mining camps scattered between Mexico and Montana. Finally in 1897, news of a great gold strike way up north in the Klondike prompted Nellie to call a halt to her adventures in the Southwest. After arranging the financing, Nellie fled the hot, dry Arizona desert to continue her endless search for the mother lode in the brutal, bone-numbing cold of the Klondike.

To reach the Klondike, Nellie had to cross the infamous Chilkoot Pass, one of the most difficult hikes in mining history. The steep, rocky pass, made nearly inaccessible by glaciers and seventy-foot snowfalls, was so difficult the Mounted

Police refused to allow anyone to enter the Yukon wilderness with less than a year's rations. Many who attempted the treacherous Chilkoot failed, but not gritty, fifty-three-year-old Nellie Cashman, who by then was a veteran miner with decades of prospecting experience.

Nellie made it through the Pass and arrived in Dawson ready to follow the pattern she had set long ago at nearly every mining camp in which she lived. She opened a restaurant, began staking out her claims, and contributed funds to the local hospital, the Catholic church, and the Sisters of St. Anne's hospital in Victoria. Throughout her life, Nellie's social life would revolve mainly around the activities of the church and the Sisters of St. Anne, a practice that probably enabled her to maintain her dignity and self-respect while she carried on her daily business life with drunks, gamblers, miners, and prostitutes.

Generous and compassionate though she was, Nellie had a hard side that seemed to contrast with her "angel of mercy" image. Nellie was first and foremost a miner and prospector, and she was determined to keep intruders from her claims. Feisty, aggressive, and proud, she became involved in several major lawsuits while in the Yukon. She won some cases and lost others, but whatever the outcome, Nellie made sure everyone understood that she was no pushover.

Credited with being the first woman prospector in Alaska Territory, Nellie welcomed the cold climate and found hardships in the wilderness challenging and stimulating. City life was no longer of interest to her. Instead, she chose to live far from the crowds, surrounded by the beauty of nature in a remote cabin five hundred miles from the nearest city or town.

By 1904, seven years after Nellie's arrival, mining in Dawson had peaked, and word was spreading about substantial finds farther north. Nellie chased the rumors to Fairbanks, where she opened her last business, a combination store and mining supply center. She faired well and even managed to raise funds for the local hospital and Catholic church. Things were going well, until Nellie was lured even farther north by reports of a huge strike near Nolan Creek at Coldfoot, hundreds of miles north of the Arctic Circle.

Nellie arrived at the northernmost mining camp in Alaska in 1905, one of the first prospectors to file a claim there. Coldfoot would also be the site of her last claim. Over the next two decades, Nellie staked more than twenty claims in this rugged Koyukuk country, the fulfillment of her dreams, where she personally worked her claims and organized a firm, the Midnight Sun Mining Company, with herself as trustee. She thrived in the fierce environment, living on the edge of the world with no amenities, using her survival talents and business acumen in the unusually harsh climate.

At seventy years old, Nellie was still running behind a dogsled, setting records and earning awards as "champion musher of the world" for working her dog team and sled 750 miles in seventeen days. She continued mining her sites at Coldfoot for the last twenty years of her life, still dreaming of the mother lode.

But the stamina that propelled Nellie through an incredibly rugged existence began to fade in 1924. When she became too weak to remain at her cabin in Coldfoot, she was moved to St. Joseph's Hospital in Victoria, British Columbia. A few months after her arrival she died of "unresolved pneumonia" in the care of her beloved Sisters of St. Anne in the hospital she had helped build forty years earlier. She was eighty years old.

Newspapers across North America printed obituaries about Nellie Cashman, calling her "the prospector with the big heart." The *New York Times* stressed her reputation as a "champion woman musher" and noted her service to needy miners.

Nellie's charitable heart and good works often overshadowed her long and successful mining career. But the fact remains that Nellie Cashman was a pioneer and a competent prospector who could face any challenge that man or the elements placed in her path. An item appearing in *The Daily Colonist* in Victoria, British Columbia, in 1962 reported that Nellie had earned more than $100,000 from one claim, spent every penny to buy other claims, then proceeded to give her fortunes away to broke and hungry miners.

Nellie was proud of her self-reliance and independent lifestyle, and once admitted that "it gives me a great deal of pride to go back to every place I've ever been and look folks square in the eye and know I've paid my bills and played the game like a man." A worthy statement indeed, from an Irish immigrant who began her stampede days in 1872 knowing nothing about mining. But Nellie Cashman learned more about geography, geology, and psychology with each new mining adventure, building a knowledge that enabled her to live the rugged, unconstrained lifestyle of a prospector during her fifty-three-year search for the big bonanza.

SARAH WINNEMUCCA

[1844–1891]

[W]ords have been put into my mouth
which have turned out to be nothing but idle wind.
Promises have been made to me in high places
that have not been kept, and I have had to suffer for this
in the loss of my people's confidence. . . .

—Sarah Winnemucca, 1882

ITH LONG DARK HAIR blowing like a banner in the wind, the buckskin-clad figure rode her horse across the barren valley. Suddenly, the earth beneath her began rumbling with the sound of hoofbeats. Turning in her saddle, she glanced over her shoulder to see a man on horseback galloping toward her.

An excellent horsewoman, Sarah Winnemucca could have easily outrun the approaching figure, but somehow the Paiute woman sensed that she was not in danger. She reined in her horse and waited.

Although Sarah understood and spoke English perfectly, she had difficulty absorbing the words she was hearing. Her father and several other Paiute had been captured by Bannock warriors. Sarah knew she had to do something to rescue her people, and she had to do it quickly. Sarah dug her heels into the sides of her mount and tore across the plains at full speed in the direction of the Bannock camp.

The story of Sarah Winnemucca is the tragic tale of a Paiute woman, educated in the ways of the white man, who spent her life trying to establish a peaceful coexistence between native tribes and white settlers in Nevada. In the end, Sarah would be ignored by the U.S. government and blamed by the very people she fought so hard to protect, due to injustices she was powerless to correct.

SARAH WINNEMUCCA *spent her life trying to establish peace between native tribes and white settlers in Nevada. Courtesy Nevada State Museum, Carson City, Nevada.*

Sarah Winnemucca was born in 1844 into the large, peaceful Paiute tribe, who occupied the high deserts of northwestern Nevada, northeastern California, and southeastern Oregon. A daughter and granddaughter of Paiute chiefs, Sarah was named Thocmetony (Shell Flower) by the Paiute. Her grandfather, Chief Truckee, had befriended Captain John Fremont and his men and led them across the Great Basin to California in the early nineteenth century. From this experience, Chief Truckee developed a high regard for whites and a belief in the brotherhood of man. But Sarah's father, Chief Winnemucca, held an opposite opinion of the whites, mistrusting them and preferring to keep his distance.

In 1850, when Sarah was six years old, her grandfather led a group of Paiute to California to learn about the ways of the whites. The group found employment as ranch hands and domestics at a large ranch near the San Joaquin River. The white ranch owners found it difficult to pronounce Thocmetony, so the young Paiute girl was renamed Sarah. Afraid of whites at first, Sarah soon became fascinated by them.

After a few months, the Paiute had seen enough of the white man's ways and returned home. Chief Truckee suspected that the whites would someday rule the land, and he wanted his beloved granddaughter to understand their ways and learn to live like them. His suspicion became evident a year later, when the Paiute became an obstacle in the path of gold seekers bound for California.

Some of the white settlers from the East stopped in Nevada territory and began establishing communities in the Paiute homeland. Chief Truckee, anxious about preparing his granddaughter for the future, arranged for thirteen-year-old Sarah to move into the home of a prominent Mormon family to learn more about the ways of the whites. Wearing calico dresses and high button shoes, Sarah was introduced to the tastes, style, and manners of the white world, and learned to read, write, and speak English and Spanish. She was treated well by her kind white hosts, but when hostilities began erupting elsewhere between white settlers and the Paiute, Sarah was summoned home.

During this turbulent time, Sarah's grandfather became gravely ill and insisted that Sarah be sent to a convent school in San Jose, California. The tribe agreed to grant the final wish of the chief, who died believing a good education would equip his beloved granddaughter with the tools to live like the white people he trusted.

Sarah was sixteen when she arrived with her sister at the Convent of Notre Dame in San Jose, the only Indians who ever attempted to enroll. Sarah later wrote in her autobiography that it was the happiest period in her life, living like a white, studying academics, and learning to create fancy needlework. Her pleasant days at the convent would be cut short, however, when some wealthy San Francisco matrons objected to Indian students. Sarah, believing her grandfather's words about the value of an education, became determined to continue her studies on her own.

Back home, Sarah found white settlers demanding more Paiute land and her people unhappy. She began selling her needlework to buy books, hoping to gain the necessary knowledge to help her people. Sarah felt that her exposure to white culture and an education would give her the means to communicate with both races about striving for a peaceful coexistence.

Sarah was proud of her Paiute heritage, but there was much about the white culture that she admired. Her sister had already lost interest in Paiute ways and chose to stay in California to live with a white family. Sarah encouraged her people to follow the whites' tradition and learn to work for a living.

But Sarah's words of peaceful coexistence would fall on deaf ears. Attacks and hostilities continued, resulting in the establishment of a temporary reservation for the Paiute on Pyramid Lake near Reno in 1860. The reservation system did not end the conflict, but Sarah was impressed by the respect shown for her people by the U.S. military. She became a translator for the army, confident that her position would bring about positive changes as she negotiated treaties and reservation policies between her people and the military.

As the encroachment of white settlers continued on former Paiute homeland, Sarah became more determined than ever to defend her people. Through her job with the army, she discovered corrupt Indian agents who robbed supplies intended for natives and caused many of her people to die from disease or starvation. Sarah began writing to government officials in Washington about the unfair practices and spoke out about the plight of her people to all who would listen.

Sarah matured into a beautiful, eloquent woman, able to communicate easily with whites and native tribes. She cut an exotic figure in a dark waistcoat and long flared skirt, with long black hair trailing down her back as she delivered impassioned accounts of the abuses suffered by her people. When her speeches began drawing crowds, relations between the government and the native tribes improved, and the Paiute were given a new reservation with neat rows of canvas tents, adequate food, and occasional work assignments.

Proud as Sarah was of her Paiute blood, she couldn't forget the more civilized life of the whites. Her words, "I would rather be with my people, but not to live as they live," summed up her ambivalent feelings. Although she may have preferred the life of a white woman in a home with pictures on the wall, Sarah was determined to fight for her people. Having a foot in each world created problems for Sarah, one of which was finding a suitable husband. She found that white men didn't seem interested in marriage to a Paiute woman, and the eligible men in her tribe were uneducated.

CHIEF WINNEMUCCA *was captured by the Bannock Indians in 1878.* SARAH *led the Paiutes, and her father, out of captivity, earning the title Queen of the Paiutes. Courtesy Nevada State Museum, Carson City, Nevada.*

The dilemma was solved a year later when a handsome young lieutenant named Edward Bartlett rode into her life. Impressed by Sarah's intelligence and native beauty, he married her in a simple ceremony in Salt Lake City, Utah.

Unfortunately, Sarah's dashing new husband was also a drunk and a scoundrel, who sold her jewelry and drained her small savings. When Chief Winnemucca heard of the marriage, he accused Sarah of dishonoring the Paiute by marrying outside of her race and demanded that she return home to her people. Following her father's timely advice, Sarah returned to Nevada.

At Fort McDermitt, Sarah found work as an interpreter for the Bureau of Indian Affairs. Proud of her job, she dressed in the tailored suits of a white woman and enjoyed the luxury of having her own room. Conditions at the fort would go well, until President Grant put an end to treaties with the Indians and declared them wards of the government, assigned to live on the reservations. Sarah's dream of a better life for her people began to crumble.

Although Congress passed an act promising reparations and ordered a stop to the violence, the exploitation of native tribes continued. Because Washington, D.C., was far from Nevada, government orders were either ignored or disobeyed. While Sarah held to her nonviolent beliefs and continued her fight with words, the starving Paiutes spoke of war.

Sarah moved to a new reservation, where she became an interpreter for the Bureau of Indian Affairs, and her people followed. Agent Sam Parrish opened a school for the children, and the Paiute were given individual plots of land. They learned to dig irrigation ditches, cut rails for fences, and plant their own crops. The Paiutes were finally content with life on the reservation, until Parrish was replaced by a corrupt new agent.

When he closed the school and reclaimed the plots of land, Sarah tried reasoning with her new boss. Pleas ignored, Sarah sent off a full report to Washington, an action that resulted in her dismissal, with orders to leave the reservation or go to prison. The angry Paiute blamed Sarah for their miserable treatment.

In 1878, U.S. troops informed Sarah that the Bannock Indians had captured her father, Chief Winnemucca, because of the tribe's assistance to white men. Enraged, Sarah joined the troops and made plans to free her people. Disguised as a Bannock "squaw," Sarah cleverly led the Paiutes out of captivity, earning the title Queen of the Paiute from her grateful father.

Sarah assisted the army through the rest of the Bannock War, serving as scout, medic, and interpreter. Afterward, the government rewarded her service by declaring the Paiute to be prisoners of war, ordering them to the Yakima Reservation in Washington Territory. Sarah gallantly tried to defend her people with protests, but again she was ignored. In January 1879, the Paiute began their tragic trek to Yakima, a three-hundred-mile bone-chilling march in mid-winter that resulted in the deaths of many women and children.

Angered by the cruel treatment and constant relocation of her people by unscrupulous agents, Sarah launched an ambitious campaign against the injustices inflicted on her people. Traveling the West Coast, she spoke movingly of broken promises to the Paiute people. With her dignified manner, eloquence, and fame from the Bannock War, Sarah became somewhat of a celebrity. In her fringed buckskin dress, bright red leggings, and a scarlet crown with eagle feathers, Sarah looked very much like the "Indian princess" the newspapers claimed she was. She spoke to capacity audiences and circulated petitions requesting humane army officers instead of dishonest Indian agents, persevering even when she was accused by a corrupt agent of being a liar and woman of questionable virtue.

Sarah's relentless claims of corruption eventually led to a federal investigation and an invitation for her to come to Washington, D.C., to voice her complaints. When Sarah, her father, and brother arrived at the nation's capitol, they were held under tight security, with no reporters allowed near them. Sarah indignantly informed her captors that she would indeed have her say.

Not wanting a scene, the government promised to grant her wishes and allow the Paiute to return safely to the Malheur Reservation. They promised to send one hundred tents and food for her people if Sarah left Washington quietly. The promises were recorded on an official document signed by Secretary of the Interior Carl Schurz, a document that Sarah would not let out of her sight. Sarah also was invited to meet briefly with President Hayes before returning to her people to share the good news.

After waiting for two weeks at the appointed delivery point for the promised tents and food that never came, Sarah was ridiculed by her people for trusting the empty words of the whites. When Sarah wired Schurz about his unfulfilled promise, she was advised to take the official, signed document to Yakima and bring her people home.

When Sarah arrived at Yakima with the document from Washington, the agent refused to accept it. Instead he offered Sarah a job as an interpreter if she agreed to remain silent about the document. Because the agent considered the Paiute his best workers, he had no intention of giving them up.

Sarah turned down the agent's offer and tried to explain the situation to her desperate people, but the Paiute called her a traitor and feared they would never return to their homeland. Humiliated, Sarah had trusted the whites again, and her people were forced to suffer for her mistake.

Sarah's refusal of the interpreter's job at Yakima upset the agent, who fired off a letter to Schurz claiming that Sarah had misrepresented the Paiute and had been banned from the reservation. Before leaving Yakima, Sarah told the agent that hell must be full of Christians like him. With no money and no place to go, Sarah contacted a trusted friend, General O. O. Howard, who arranged for her to teach the children of the Bannock prisoners at Vancouver.

In 1881, when Sarah was thirty-seven, she married Lewis Hopkins, another white man, who gambled away the money she had earned in Vancouver. Hopkins preferred unemployment, so the couple returned to the Indian way of life on the reservation, where they found the Paiute working the land and the agent reaping the harvest.

Weary of false promises and the miserable conditions of her people, Sarah decided to take her case again before the American people. In 1883, with little money and very few friends, thirty-nine-year-old Sarah left Nevada with her husband to take her message to the East Coast.

Fortune was destined to shine on Sarah in Boston, where she met two wealthy and influential sisters, Elizabeth Peabody and Mary Mann, the widow of educator Horace Mann. The sisters were impressed with Sarah's persuasive pleas for her people and generously assisted Sarah at her lectures. They also encouraged her to write a book, which they promised to edit and publish.

Sarah, the first Native American woman to write a book, drew thousands of people on the East Coast to her lectures. They came to hear her speak and have her sign copies of her autobiography, *Life Among the Piutes, Their Wrongs and Claims*, in which she exposed the injustices against her people and the double-dealing and corruption of the agents. When an unscrupulous agent made a desperate effort to counteract Sarah's indictments of him with a story that she was a veteran of a Nevada bordello, the indignant Bostonians sent letters refuting the charges and vouched for Sarah's character and patriotic contributions. Later five thousand people signed a petition requesting that Indians be given lands and citizen's rights, and legislation was prepared.

In the spring of 1884, Sarah and a group of distinguished Easterners appeared before a Congressional committee and spoke for the bill, which was passed later in Congress. When Sarah returned home to Nevada, she was a heroine and the most popular "Indian" in the country. With her father Chief Winnemucca now dead, Sarah was the leader and "mother" of her people.

Believing Congress to be the nation's ultimate authority, Sarah must have been appalled when Secretary of the Interior Schurz resented her indictment of his department and refused to implement the legislation. The new Congress did not force the issue, so time would pass before the Paiute were allowed to return to their homeland. Sarah's courageous campaign ultimately did end the despicable forced transfers, but her people were too weary to be grateful. With spirits shattered by too many broken promises, the Paiute accused Sarah of collusion with the U.S. government and blamed their hardships on her.

The last bright spot in Sarah's life appeared when Senator Leland Stanford, founder of Stanford University in California, awarded Sarah and her brother Natchez 160 acres of land near Lovelock, Nevada. Natchez farmed his share of land, while Sarah opened a school for native children. After a few years, Sarah closed the school to care for her husband, who was dying from tuberculosis. When her own health began to fail from the same disease, Sarah moved to Idaho to spend her last days living quietly with her sister. She died on October 14, 1891, at age forty-seven.

Generations would pass before Sarah Winnemucca would be honored for her relentless efforts to bridge the worlds of her people and the white settlers. But her legacy is treasured today at the reservation at Pyramid Lake, where Paiute are more likely to file a lawsuit than weave baskets. They have survived court battles and protests against government agencies, and they have increased their land holdings. Sarah Winnemucca would be proud.

LOTTA CRABTREE

[1847–1924]

*At the age of eight, little Lotta Crabtree
earned more money in one night entertaining miners than her
father had made in four years working the mines.
Lotta's gold-studded career whisked the
saucy little comedienne from the rough-and-tumble
stages of the mining camps to the
celebrated theaters of San Francisco, New York, and London.*

*T*HE HORDES OF HOPEFUL TRAVELERS driven west in 1849 by promises of plentiful gold nuggets just waiting for the picking were called the "forty-niners." Most were men who made the journey alone, leaving families and comforts behind. Once they arrived in the West, they faced long, lonely days digging in the dirt, disappointed and hungry for their families and a little diversion.

When performers began making the rounds at mining camps in the first days of the gold rush, they discovered that miners were an eager audience and generous in their appreciation. For years, the traveling acts that provided the miners with entertainment were more of the circus-act variety, a bear-versus-bull fight, and the occasional singing balladeer. But by the early 1850s, the entertainment companies had discovered that what the miners responded to most generously were comedy acts and romantic, nostalgic songs.

In 1853, a group of California forty-niners would discover in their midst a sparkling gem of another sort, a lovable, pint-sized comedienne named Lotta Crabtree. Eager for music, laughter, and the memories of home that Lotta sparked, the miners showered the little performer with sacks of gold dust, signaling Lotta's manager-mother that she had finally struck the big bonanza.

LOTTA CRABTREE *grew up to be the best-known comedienne of her time.*
Courtesy San Francisco Performing Arts Library & Museum.

The petite, perky moppet, who grew up to be the best-known comedienne of her time, was born in New York in 1847. She was named Charlotte Mignon Crabtree and was called Lotta. Both of her parents were English immigrants; her mother, Mary Ann, was an upholsterer, and her father, John Ashworth Crabtree, was a bookseller.

By 1851, John Crabtree could no longer resist the promise of fortunes to be made in the goldfields of California, and he made up his mind to join the rush to the West. He sold his bookstore, packed his bags, and promised to send for his wife and daughter soon. Several months passed before Mary Ann received instructions to meet her husband in San Francisco. Gathering up four-year-old Lotta, she traveled by steamship the lengthy route around Cape Horn to San Francisco, only to find that John Crabtree had moved on.

Mary Ann managed to find living quarters for herself and Lotta with friends in the city and became involved with a troupe of traveling actors and actresses, which included popular child performers called "fairy stars." When Mary Ann Crabtree heard how much money the young entertainers earned, she promptly enrolled Lotta in dancing class.

A year later, John Crabtree finally sent word to his family, inviting them to join him in Grass Valley, California. Prospecting hadn't turned up any gold yet for Crabtree, so he established a boardinghouse for miners. When the family was together again, he turned over operation of the business to Mary Ann and went back to prospecting.

A few doors down the street from the boardinghouse lived the exotic Lola Montez, a notorious actress who had selected Grass Valley for her brief sabbatical from the stage. She soon became friends with the Crabtree family and formed a special relationship with petite, red-haired Lotta. The charming little girl with the snapping dark eyes and merry laugh adored Lola and became her protégée, dressing up in her costumes and dancing to her German music box. Lola tucked Lotta firmly under her wing and taught her to sing small ballads and to perform special dance steps in ballet, fandango, and the highland fling. She also taught Lotta how to ride on horseback, and they often rode trails in the area together.

Occasionally Lola would coax Lotta into performing before a small crowd that had gathered on a street corner in town, and she beamed with pride at the child's talents. The coaching of little Lotta is said to have been Lola Montez's greatest contribution to American theater, as her petite protégée one day became America's top comedienne. Mary Ann was aware of the attention showered on her daughter by the famous celebrity, and was convinced that her Lotta was brimming with talent. She knew she had to get Lotta on the stage.

John Crabtree, meanwhile, was becoming frustrated in Grass Valley, an area that hadn't produced the desired results. He moved his family forty miles north to the mining community of Rabbit Creek (La Porte) and looked for another boardinghouse to open. Mary Ann began to scout around for dancing and singing lessons for Lotta.

She soon found a teacher, a young Italian musician named Matt Taylor, who ran a saloon and a little log theater. A dancer, he also ran a dancing school for children in the camp, specializing in jigs and reels, which Lotta would add to her growing repertoire. One night, a popular fairy star arrived at Taylor's small log theater and attempted to put on a show. Taylor had to refuse since it was the evening he had selected for the debut of a new fairy star, Lotta Crabtree. He sent the young traveling performer across the street to another building and prepared for Lotta's big night.

Mary Ann Crabtree, who planned to keep a tight rein on her daughter's upcoming career, became Lotta's manager. Aware that Irish blood flowed through the veins of many area miners, she decided on a program of Irish entertainment for Lotta's debut. Using her sewing skills, she whipped up a colorful Gaelic costume for Lotta, featuring a tiny green coat with tails, knee breeches, and a high green hat.

With a shillelagh in her hand, tiny Lotta appeared on stage looking like a petite Irish sprite, with her broad smile, bouncing red curls, and sparkling dark eyes announcing to all that she was delighted to be there. The friendly, familiar faces staring back gave her a comfortable feeling, and she began a set of jigs and reels, smiling and laughing merrily while she danced. The natural, infectious enjoyment she displayed during her performances enchanted her audience and became one of Lotta's most powerful success secrets.

For her debut's finale, Lotta appeared in a stunning white dress and sang the familiar, sentimental ballad, "How Can I leave Thee?" It was the perfect choice, and her final bows were followed by tears and cheers from the appreciative audience, which included those who had come over from the rival show across the street. The stage was showered with dollars, pesos, gold nuggets, bags of gold dust, and a fifty-dollar gold slug, all of which Mary Ann Crabtree hastily collected in her apron. In one night, eight-year-old Lotta Crabtree, who looked more like a six-year-old, earned more money than her father had in his past four years of prospecting. The evening also marked the launching of one of the nineteenth century's most spectacular careers.

With her mother in tow, the petite, copper-haired Lotta began traveling as a member of Taylor's young troupe, the Metropolitan Company. She sang and

LOTTA CRABTREE, *approximately 1865 at age 18. Courtesy San Francisco Performing Arts Library & Museum.*

danced into the hearts of the generous miners in towns and camps all over the West. Lotta performed jigs, flings, polkas, and a variety of musical acts that she had picked up from other traveling professionals. She learned the intricate steps of a soft-shoe dance from a touring black dancer, and the popular wandering minstrels taught Lotta how to blacken her face and play the banjo, skills that she added to a versatile program.

Taylor's troupe traveled at night, by horseback or on mules, sleeping upright in saddles, a canvas tent, a cheap boardinghouse, or on the ground under the stars. They paraded into each new town and camp behind their leader, Taylor, who announced their arrival on his drum. The young performers would appear on makeshift stages in saloons and basements or on street corners, playing to small, captive audiences that provided Lotta with an opportunity to hone her talents.

From the small crowds that gathered to watch the performances, Lotta learned how to please the audience. She discovered which steps sparked a cheer and whether to dance in a delicate, graceful manner or with comical romps and stomps. Lotta performed a variety of roles, dressed in colorful costumes created by her mother's expert hands. She played Topsy, an Irish leprechaun, a Cockney lad, a Scot lassie, and an American sailor, and the audience adored and rewarded her. After her performance, Lotta would run out and collect the assortment of coins, nuggets, and baubles and stuff them into her shoe for her mother's safekeeping.

In 1856, the Crabtree family moved back to San Francisco. By this time, Lotta and Mary Ann had completed five years of touring with Taylor and his company. Mary Ann organized a traveling tour for Lotta to northern California's frontier towns, returning to San Francisco during the winter months so Lotta could study voice and piano. They dreamed of the day Lotta would perform in a high-class, legitimate theater.

Lotta's break soon came in a variety show at a rundown theater on the San Francisco waterfront. But as she had since the beginning, Lotta stole the show and soon became a popular act at variety halls and amusement parks all over the area. She was also the youngest member of the cast, and earned the title "Miss Lotta, the San Francisco Favorite," before she had reached her teens.

Occasionally Lotta would develop a case of stage fright, but with a bit of coaxing from her mother, she would bounce onto the stage as a professional. Although Mary Ann Crabtree had all the traits of a quintessential stage mother, she proved to be a shrewd businesswoman and manager. Suspicious of banks and paper money, Mary Ann insisted on transporting all of Lotta's earnings (nuggets and coins) in a big leather satchel. When the case became too heavy to carry, Mary Ann had the loot transferred to a huge steamer trunk. Considering all the traveling they did, it is amazing they were never robbed of their small fortune.

Mary Ann maintained a close watch over her daughter, allowing her very few diversions and no social life. In 1864, after Lotta had performed for ten years without stop in the West, Mary Ann decided to launch a tour in the East. She arranged for seventeen-year-old Lotta to perform on stages in New York, Boston, Chicago, and other Midwestern cities. Lotta arrived in New York during the Civil War years, a time when business was notoriously bad. But at the theater in New York City where Lotta made her debut, she performed in front of a full house for her entire six-week run. The *Clipper* reported that no other star had achieved such a triumph.

When the shrewd Mary Ann began taking advantage of the new mass-market newspapers, Lotta's career took a giant leap. At the top theaters in the East, Lotta appeared in familiar plays like *Uncle Tom's Cabin* and the romping *Pet of the Petticoats*, where her performance of Irish songs, Irish jigs, and banjo tunes thrilled the audience. Lotta became a wildly popular actress and comedienne and a darling of the media, who often featured stories about her romances. They weren't true, of course, because Mary Ann discouraged any close relationships for her daughter and made sure that Lotta's life contained little else than the theater and her family.

Lotta's greatest success came when she played the starring role in *Little Nell and the Marchioness*, written for her by England's popular author, Charles Dickens. Afterwards, the versatile Lotta had her choice of top roles and performed at the very best theaters. Although she won raves for her tragic roles, Lotta preferred comedy. She liked breaking traditions with her short skirts and daring antics, shocking the audience by wearing men's clothes and smoking the rolled black cigars that would become her trademark and a habit that she continued offstage.

She also enjoyed playing the part of a coquette in melodramas that featured lots of singing and dancing. In *The Little Detective*, the versatile Lotta played the roles of six characters, a performance that allowed her to use her complete repertoire.

For twenty years, Lotta Crabtree reigned as one of the most popular actresses on the American stage. She became the most celebrated comedienne of her era and the highest-paid performer on Broadway. In 1870, when Lotta was twenty-three, she started her own company rather than tour with the usual local stock, and produced such hits as *Pointe Lynde Light*, *Musette*, and *Mamizelle Nitouche*.

Although the press continued to link her with many gentlemen, Lotta never married. With a busy career and a mother-manager allowing little time for social life, the trim, petite Lotta continued to play children's roles and youthful roles well into her forties.

The money kept flowing in, and Mary Ann managed it well. When the steamer trunks became to heavy to move, Mary Ann invested in local real estate, bonds, and other opportunities. She continued to oversee Lotta's affairs, booking plays, selecting locations, and organizing acting troupes. She also arranged trips abroad for the family, which now included Lotta's two younger brothers. During a tour of England, Lotta performed in the country's top theaters. She also studied French, visited museums, and learned to paint, an interest that she pursued for the rest of her life.

After a European holiday in 1892, Lotta retired at age of forty-five. She moved to New Jersey with her mother, and she bought a cottage on a lake, which she named Attol Tryst (Lotta spelled backwards). She kept horses, continued to paint, and smoked her trademark black cigars.

When Mary Ann Crabtree died in 1905, Lotta was left with a fortune provided by her mother's wise real estate investments. She led a comfortable, if somewhat reclusive life, with occasional appearances at charity benefits, eventually moving to Boston, where she bought a hotel.

In 1875 Lotta presented the city of San Francisco with a thirty-five-foot iron statue, located at the intersection of Kearney and Market Streets. She returned again to the city she loved in 1915, forty years later, to make her final public appearance on Lotta Crabtree Day at the San Francisco Panama-Pacific Exposition.

Lotta lived the last years of her life at her hotel in Boston, until her death in 1924 at the age of seventy-seven. The bulk of her estate, estimated at a whopping $4 million, was left to veterans, aging actors, students of music, and animals. Her will was contested, but after a two-year court battle, it remained intact as Lotta had dictated. She was buried next to her mother in Woodlawn Cemetery in New York City, far from her Wild West origins.

Lotta Crabtree's remarkable life is worth remembering for her incredible success at creating a celebrity image that delighted Victorian audiences in the East, even though this child of the gold rush learned to perform in the rough, rugged mining camps of the Far West.

MARTHA HUGHES
CANNON

[*1857–1932*]

This highly educated physician, politician, suffragist,
and first woman in the country to serve as a state senator
fled to Europe to live in exile rather than testify
against her polygamous husband, with whom she and their
children were never allowed to live publicly as a family.

O F THE MANY LOFTY GOALS Martha Hughes Cannon set for herself in life, she reached most of them. She earned multiple college degrees and became a physician, nursing school founder, and suffragist, and was elected the first female state senator in Utah and in the United States. But the one goal this dynamic, determined woman would never attain was to live as wife with her beloved husband and father of their three children. Instead the intelligent, accomplished Dr. Cannon chose to go "underground" and into exile in England in order to save her husband from federal prosecution.

Although the location of Cannon's exile may have been far from her home in the Salt Lake Valley, it wasn't far from Llandudno, Wales, where Martha "Mattie" Hughes was born in 1857. One year later, the Hughes family, who had been converted to the Church of Jesus Christ of Latter-day Saints by Mormon missionaries from the United States, immigrated to the U.S. After spending two years in New York nursing Mr. Hughes, who was in poor health, the family journeyed westward across the country to join the Mormon community in Utah Territory.

By the time she was five years old, Mattie had already completed an ocean voyage and a difficult three-and-a-half-month cross-country journey by covered wagon. During the rugged trek west she witnessed her sister's death, and shortly after the family arrived in Utah Territory in 1861, her father died. These two tragedies, which Mattie was unable to prevent or alter, inflamed her with the desire to become a physician.

MARTHA HUGHES CANNON *was the first woman ever to hold the office of State Senator in the United States. Courtesy Utah State Historical Society.*

After the family had settled in the Salt Lake Valley, Mattie's mother married James Patton Paul, with whom she had five more children. Mattie grew close to her stepfather and shared with him her hopes of becoming a doctor, an ambition he encouraged.

A serious, industrious child, Mattie remained focused on her dream of attending medical school, knowing she would have to work hard to reach her goal. She began teaching elementary school when she was fourteen and worked as a typesetter for the *Deseret News* and the *Women's Exponent* to support her education later at the University of Deseret (now the University of Utah).

After graduation from the University of Deseret with a degree in chemistry in 1875, Mattie attended medical school at the University of Michigan, where her impressive credentials earned her an acceptance without an interview. In medical school, Mattie was an independent and practical student and also a bit bizarre. She ignored convention by wearing her hair unfashionably short, clomping around in men's boots with her skirts pinned up for the fourteen-block march to work through snow and slush. With her frugal living habits, part-time jobs, and perseverance, Mattie was able to earn her medical degree by the time she was twenty-three.

Before returning home to Salt Lake City, Mattie accumulated more academic degrees. In 1882 she would be the only woman in a class of seventy-five to earn a bachelor of science degree from the University of Pennsylvania's School of Pharmacy. She hoped to strengthen her speaking skills on public-health issues, so she also earned a bachelor of oratory degree from the National School of Elocution and Oratory.

Armed with a fistful of degrees, twenty-five-year-old Mattie Hughes returned to Salt Lake City, where she established Utah's first training school for nurses, taught classes in nursing and obstetrics, and opened her own medical office. She then became the second resident physician at the new Deseret Hospital, where she worked from 1882 to 1886.

One day when Dr. Mattie Hughes was washing down the hospital's front porch, an obstacle appeared in her cleaning path. Irritated, Mattie ordered the distinguished-looking gentleman to move aside. The man became indignant, but Mattie held her ground until Angus M. Cannon, the superintendent of the hospital, obeyed her command and moved out of the way. Superintendent Cannon, who was also the president of the Salt Lake City stake of the Mormon Church, had just met his next wife.

When Martha Maria Hughes married Angus Munn Cannon, twenty-three years her senior, on October 6, 1884, she became the fourth of Cannon's six wives. This plural marriage would bring an avalanche of uncertainty and

MARTHA *became* ANGUS MUNN CANNON's *fourth of six wives. Courtesy Utah State Historical Society.*

depression into the life of a normally focused, confident woman. The trouble would start not long after the marriage, when Angus was put in prison for the practice of polygamy.

The custom of polygamy, of a man having plural wives, incited a great deal of anti-Mormon hostility, which escalated in the late nineteenth century with a national crusade. Anti-polygamists denounced the practice in the name of women's rights. They claimed that plural marriages enslaved women, even though Utah's Mormon women, who had been granted suffrage in 1870, had made no attempt over the years to reform marriage and end polygamy.

Mormon women defended polygamy for the same reason as their anti-polygamy opponents—women's rights. They claimed that plural marriages guaranteed a woman the right to marry and bear children, and that it also controlled male immorality. The fact that plural marriage was a requirement for advancement in the church hierarchy made it a common practice among the church elite, although most Mormon marriages were monogamous.

1896 Senate Members. Courtesy Utah State Historical Society.

Mormon women, like the rest of the women in Utah, had been granted full citizenship in 1870, decades before their sisters all across the nation would be allowed to vote. Utah's support for suffrage can be traced to the state's early Mormon settlers, who had followed their leader, Brigham Young, westward to the Salt Lake Valley beginning in 1847. By granting women the right to vote, Mormons hoped to establish a voting majority against non-Mormon settlers, who were arriving by the wagonload or on the recently completed transcontinental railroad. Mormon men were not threatened by women's suffrage, since they were confident that Mormon women approved of plural marriage, a situation they hoped would disprove critics' claim that polygamy enslaved women.

But the anti-polygamy crusade would not be stopped, and the relentless attacks against plural marriage continued. Campaigns were launched against the "twin relics of barbarism —polygamy and slavery," which led to legislation penalizing polygamists with fines, political disenfranchisement, and prison sentences. Unlawful cohabitation was also banned, making plural wives criminals along with their polygamist husbands, and making any children born to such a union after 1883 illegitimate. In 1887 Congress passed the Edmunds-Tucker Act, requiring plural wives to testify against their husbands. For Dr. Mattie

Hughes Cannon, a plural wife married for three years and now pregnant with her first child, the new legislation presented a dilemma. Should she stay hidden underground or escape into exile?

With federal marshals hunting for Cannon with a warrant for her arrest, Mattie hastily arranged a statewide inspection tour of nurses' training schools, then fled the city. When she returned to Salt Lake City, she stayed hidden in the underground Mormon network and gave birth to her daughter, Elizabeth Rachel. Mattie was determined to avoid testifying against her husband and furnishing proof of their polygamous marriage, and as a physician who had delivered the babies of other plural marriage partners, she did not want to testify against them or others in the same position.

Mattie continued to avoid arrest, living like a mole underground and traveling incognito with her baby, hidden beneath a pile of straw in the bottom of a sheep wagon. She wrote to her husband, "I grow heartily sick and disgusted with it—polygamy." Finally, when the situation became too confining, Cannon decided to flee with her baby into exile in England, claiming, "I would rather be a stranger in a strange land than to be a sneaking captive at home."

During her two years of self-imposed exile in England, where Mattie and her daughter lived with relatives, Mattie and Angus exchanged many letters. At the beginning, she viewed her situation as an exciting adventure. "Were it all written or told . . . [i]t would make as thrilling a tale as ever appeared on the pages of fiction." As time wore on, despite her love for her husband, she began to suffer from the strain of separation and insecurity, writing letters that exposed her loneliness and anguish. Struggling between her head and her heart regarding the subject of polygamy, she wrote to Angus, "Oh for a home! A husband of my own because he is my own. A father for my children whom they know by association. And all the little auxiliaries that make life worth the living. Will they ever be enjoyed by this storm-tossed exile? Or must life thus drift on and one more victim swell the ranks of the great unsatisfied!"

A combination of poor health, unpredictable finances, childbirth, and exile eventually took their toll on Cannon, and she would be forced to ask her husband for money he was unable to provide. In 1888, Mattie returned to Salt Lake City, where she lived with her parents, reopened her medical practice, and taught nursing and obstetrics classes. Dr. Mattie Hughes Cannon became a prominent member of the community, but she was never able to live openly as the wife of Angus Cannon, even though they produced three children.

Along with making plural marriage a crime, the Edmunds-Tucker Act had disenfranchised Utah women seventeen years after they had won the right to vote and hold public office. Mattie soon became actively involved in local suffrage efforts to help Utah women win back the vote. She also joined the national suffrage movement and traveled to Washington, D.C., to speak before Congress on suffrage efforts.

In 1890, the Mormon Church issued the declaration that the church had forbidden the practice of polygamy. Five years later Utah was granted statehood and its women were granted suffrage again. It was also the year before Mattie Cannon became famous throughout Utah and the nation as the first woman elected to a state senate. But Mattie began making headlines even before she was elected.

Utah's first election as a state in 1896 was a much-publicized affair. The respected Dr. Mattie Hughes Cannon was one of five Democrats running "at large" for state senator from Salt Lake County. Among the five Republican candidates running at large for the same position was her husband, Angus.

Local newspapers had a field day with stories of the upcoming election. The *Salt Lake Herald*, a Democratic newspaper, said, "Mrs. Mattie Hughes Cannon . . . is the better man of the two. Send Mrs. Cannon to the State Senate and let Mr. Cannon, as a Republican, remain at home to manage home industry."

When Mattie Hughes Cannon defeated her husband by 2,671 votes, the newspapers printed stories about "a leading Mormon polygamist who was defeated by his fourth wife." Her election to the state senate in 1896 earned Cannon the distinction of being the first woman ever to hold that office in the United States.

Cannon served two terms as state senator. During her first term, she intro-duced three bills that became law. One provided education for those with hearing, speech, and sight impairments; the second bill created a seven-member state board of health; and the third relieved working conditions for women sales clerks by providing chairs, stools, and other resting aids for those periods when they were not working. With her medical background, Cannon took a primary interest in public health. She led the movement to correct problems of sanitation and disease in Utah and to abolish the unsanitary practice of attaching tin cups to public drinking fountains.

Cannon's second term in the senate ended with the birth of her third child, Gwendolyn, three weeks after adjournment. When her second term was over, the *Deseret News* wrote: "In political conventions, her wit, rapid thinking, and knowledge made her capable of holding her own and of representing her sex most favorably."

After serving in the senate, Cannon joined the Utah Board of Health and `the Utah State School for Speech and Hearing. Later, she retired officially from public and political life but never fully reestablished her medical practice. As a

Utah State Capitol. Courtesy Utah State Historical Society.

medical doctor, the petite Cannon was remembered most for her skills as an obstetrician with tiny hands that enabled her to maneuver babies easily during childbirth.

When Angus Cannon died in 1915 in Salt Lake City, Mattie began dividing her time between Salt Lake City and Los Angeles. In 1924, she moved permanently to California to live in a home built by her son and his family, and to work at Graves Medical Clinic. Martha Hughes Cannon died of cancer in 1932 at age seventy-five in Los Angeles, seventeen years after the death of Angus Munn Cannon. Angus and Mattie are buried near each other in the Salt Lake Cemetery.

The roles in Cannon's life were multiple and often at odds. She was a faithful follower of the Mormon Church, a physician, a plural wife, suffragist, exile, fugitive, the first female state senator in the country, and a single mother of three for most of her children's growing years. Life was often difficult for this strong-willed woman, who began making her mark on the Western landscape before women in the East had won the right to vote.

MAY ARKWRIGHT HUTTON

[1860–1915]

Big, bold, brassy, and brave,
May Arkwright Hutton rose from rags to riches
on the sheer force of her personality, spirit,
and dream of striking it rich in the silver fields of Idaho.

PEN THIS DAMNED DOOR or I'll have your hide," bellowed the booming voice on the other side of the huge wooden door now being battered by bangs, thumps, and kicks. When the soldier lifted the heavy bar, a hefty, red-faced May Hutton plowed into the "bull pen" in search of her husband. When she spotted him on a straw-filled bunk in the crude, makeshift prison, she became even more outraged at finding her sweet, gentle Al imprisoned like a common criminal.

"Utterly outrageous, a flagrant violation of human rights," roared May. "Al, you and all the rest of the card-carrying union miners don't have to worry. Big May Hutton's alerting the press and every official worth reaching. You'll see, I'll have you outta here in no time, or, believe me, I'll make them sweat!"

Two weeks later, Al Hutton was free to return home to May, and soon afterward the rest of the imprisoned miners were released and the government troops sent back to their base. May Arkwright Hutton, built like a battleship with a personality to match, had saved the day again.

Although she charged through much of her adult life like a tank in battle, May arrived in Idaho in the early 1880s armed only with her dream of striking it rich. A formidable and courageous woman, she refused to abandon the dream and was rewarded for her persistence. She also found in the American Northwest a stage on which to champion the two great causes of her life—labor unions and women's suffrage.

MAY ARKWRIGHT HUTTON *arrived in Idaho in the early 1880s. Courtesy Northwest Museum of Arts & Culture, Eastern Washington State Historical Society, Spokane, Washington.*

May Arkwright was born in 1860 in Mahoning County, Ohio, to parents who reportedly abandoned their illegitimate daughter in her infancy. She lived with her blind grandfather until she was ten years old, receiving only three years of schooling. While still a young girl, May started working in a boardinghouse and was able to observe the dreary life of the coal miners in the area. Depressed by their hopeless condition, she yearned for a better life.

May matured into a large-boned, heavyset woman, plain in appearance and blunt in speech. She married a local mule driver for the mines when she was twenty-two, but was abandoned a year later, when her husband ran off with their savings and reportedly drowned. When she noticed the Northern Pacific Railroad advertisement offering "free gold for the picking in the West," May began dreaming about joining the rush. Later, when she heard about gold strikes along the North Fork of the Coeur d'Alene River, she was ready to seek her fortune in the West.

May boarded the train bound for the Idaho Panhandle in 1883 with a group of forty coal miners who shared her dream of freedom and riches. After leaving the train in Rathborn, the entourage climbed aboard a steamboat and chugged across Lake Coeur d'Alene and completed the last few miles to the Coeur d'Alene district on horseback.

When they reached their destination, a fellow traveler offered May a job at the food counter behind his saloon. May accepted and soon began working fourteen-hour days, saving money and gaining a sense of independence. A few years later, when she heard that the railroad was extending its narrow-gauge line, she decided to move on and open a place of her own. She discovered the future location of the tracks and selected a site at Wardner Junction to open a boardinghouse and dining room.

Word spread quickly about May's cooking skills, and soon her business was thriving. On Saturday, payday for the miners, May doubled up her apron and walked around the table, collecting money for the week. With a personality that matched her 225-pound frame, May had little trouble collecting what she was due.

She may never have been mistaken for a beauty, but May was a smart, shrewd, and kindhearted woman. An industrious type herself, May felt a kinship with the lonely, hard-working men she fed and wanted desperately to help. Her heart went out to the unfortunate ones who squandered their pay in one Saturday night at the saloon, and she pitied those who jumped from job to job, living paycheck to paycheck and selling their claims because they were too impatient to wait. May, who remained true to her dream of striking it rich, began purchasing small interests in mining ventures.

Among those who came to May's table were railroad men, like the soft-spoken engineer, Levi "Al" Hutton. Like May, Al had grown up, unwanted and poor, struggling through childhood to eventually make something of himself. Their origins were similar, but their personalities were as different as night and day. May was as opinionated and loud as Al was quiet and sober, but none of it seemed to matter when they set their wedding date for November 17, 1887.

A year later the railroad extended the track and Al was given a new route, so May closed up her boardinghouse and moved with Al to Wallace, a town on the South Fork of the Coeur d'Alene River. In this busy little town, with a government, school, church, bank, and newspaper, May and Al bought a humble two-room shack on a steep hillside above the tracks.

Without a business to run, May hoped to pursue social projects. The social set in Wallace had other ideas, however. With her huge frame, bawdy language, and outlandish clothes, May stood out like a tumbleweed in a rose garden, and her preference for ruffles and bare-necked, bosomy costumes sent shock waves through the community. But May didn't really care a whit about winning a place on the social register of this mining town; she wanted to do something important to help the struggling, underpaid miners.

May and Al's cozy house above the tracks soon became headquarters for miners and union representatives trying to get a foothold in the mines. May's tasty pies and attentive ear made her a popular figure with the labor people, and the more she listened to the miners' complaints and union promises, the more she was convinced that unions could solve the problems.

Labor problems arrived at the Wallace mines in 1892. Miners wanted an increase in their three-dollars-a-day wages to match those at a nearby unionized mine. When negotiations with mine owners failed, a group of disgruntled miners reportedly blew up a mill, killing three men and harming many others. May later wrote her own book about the incident known as the Rocky Mountain Revolution, but in the meantime union troubles boiled and bubbled for the next seven years, with May right in the thick of things.

Even with her commitment to the union, May still dreamed of striking it rich someday. She kept a sharp eye and ear tuned to investment opportunities, and when she spotted the glittering silver flecks in some ore samples spread out on her dining table, May wanted a stake in the claim. Although the Hercules Mine had been unproductive since its discovery eight years earlier, the samples encouraged the group around the table. The Huttons joined the small group of investors and bought one-sixteenth of a share in the mine for $505. They later increased their holdings to three thirty-seconds of a share for an additional $375.

Everyone with a stake in the Hercules Mine helped support the venture, a hard and painfully slow process. Four years later, it still had not produced, and spirits were sagging. When May heard that the big mining companies she held in such contempt wanted to buy them out, she became all the more determined to hold onto the claim. Then she turned her mind back onto her union crusade.

In 1899, problems arose when a large area mine closed, leaving union miners without jobs. When the mine reopened later, staffed with imported nonunion workers, May was furious. She launched a campaign and came out firing with both barrels, attacking mine owners and corporations, making impassioned speeches, and sending letters to newspaper editors in Idaho and Spokane.

Even May's peace-loving husband, Al, was involved in the commotion that erupted when the jobless union men decided to punish the mine owners for their unfair treatment. With a gun in his ribs and a train filled with an angry crowd of a thousand jobless miners, Al was instructed by the mob to drive the train to the powder house. After a highly explosive load of dynamite was loaded onto the boxcars, Al was ordered to take the overloaded train to the mine where the three thousand pounds of dynamite reduced the huge mine to ashes in three earthshaking booms.

Government troops were called in to arrest all card-carrying union miners, who were then loaded onto trains and hauled to a giant hay barn called the bull pen. May was incensed over this violation of human rights, and by the arrest and incarceration of her gentle husband. Alerting the press and every official she could reach, big May plowed into the bull pen demanding the freedom of the imprisoned men. When everything was said and done, the men were freed and the troops sent back to their base, leaving May time to plan her next project.

In the summer of 1899, the Hercules Mine investment group began work on a second tunnel. One corporation offered $6 million for the mine, but May felt sure it would yield much more someday and cautioned the investors to hold out for the big strike.

The big bonanza happened on Friday, June 13, 1901, when an ore of high-grade silver and lead was unearthed at the Hercules Mine. The *Wallace Free Press* broke the news of the lucky strike in mid-August, reporting that the Hercules ore contained nearly 38 percent silver, the most concentrated of any produced in the area. May and the little group of investors who had spent eight years picking their way through solid rock had finally struck it rich. Their mine would produce 6 percent of the lead mined in the U.S., employ eight hundred people, and produce for twenty-four years. The Hercules made millionaires out of a group of eighteen people.

No longer poor, May and Al moved from the two-room hillside shack to an elegant house in downtown Wallace. May loved to show off her new eight-bedroom, cream-colored home and entertained frequently. She relished her role as an ambassador of sorts and welcomed the politically ambitious who came through town, including Teddy Roosevelt, William Jennings Bryan, and Clarence Darrow.

Still harboring angry feelings over the newspapers' handling of the Rocky Mountain Revolution in 1892, May decided to write a book about the "true" side of the incident. In *The Coeur d'Alenes: A Tale of the Modern Inquisition in Idaho*, May claimed she was "neither miner nor mine owner and in a neutral position and able to give a true and impartial account of the events." She then proceeded to attack mine owners, state officials, and the U.S. Army. The book came out in 1900, and May found people eager to read her exposé of corporate slave drivers, making the book a great source of pride for its largely self-educated author, publisher, and promoter.

Although May lacked the culture and social skills that local society demanded, this large, boisterous, and overdressed woman eased herself into the world of the wealthy without a problem. She involved herself in fundraising efforts, community charities, and church bazaars and became a major supporter of community drama and musical events. She proudly wore her frilly, ruffled gowns to the banquets and balls at the Masonic Lodge, where Al was a member.

Now that May was in the social whirl as a rich mine owner, she needed to change her image from scrappy labor union promoter to dignified philanthropist. She feared the embarrassing and damaging effects of the book she had written against mine owners and corporations. So as quietly as possible, May collected all the books she could track down, even buying them back at inflated prices.

In 1907 the Huttons followed many of their well-heeled friends to Spokane, Washington, ninety miles away from Coeur d'Alene. Al purchased a site on one of the town's busiest corners and began work on the Hutton Block, a four-story building that would expand later by three additional floors. Most of the fourth floor was designated as living quarters for the Huttons, and May spared no expense in her attempt to transform it into the most luxurious apartment west of the Rockies. Afterwards, she was ready to tackle a problem that would rekindle the passion she once had for men and labor unions. This time the issue was women's suffrage in Washington, the state where May now lived, and where women had not yet been granted the vote.

Women's suffrage bills had been passed and repealed in the state of Washington since 1850. When women's suffrage was voted down again in 1910 after Washington was admitted to the Union, May was outraged and declared it time for women to have the vote once and for all. With renewed energy and an ambitious campaign, May Hutton was ready for battle.

She recruited champion suffragists Susan B. Anthony from the East Coast and Abigail Scott Duniway from neighboring Oregon, and took the women's suffrage crusade throughout the state. Even Emma Smith DeVoe, a national

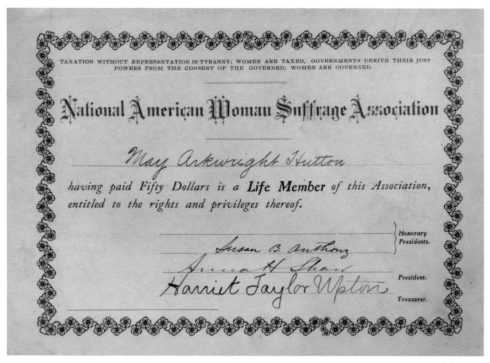

In 1910 MAY *declared it time for women to have the vote once and for all. Courtesy Northwest Museum of Arts & Culture, Eastern Washington State Historical Society, Spokane, Washington.*

organizer from Chicago, came to help, suggesting an educational campaign for women. But May insisted on a more vigorous suffrage crusade. The difference of opinion and philosophy between the two determined suffragists resulted in a divided campaign, with May championing women's suffrage in the eastern part of the state and DeVoe working in the west.

May organized a large delegation from Spokane to go to Seattle to meet with the Washington Equal Suffrage Association. When she was refused admission to the convention for keeping the dues and identity of the delegates secret, a clamor followed that ended with a call to the police and an indignant May Hutton barging across the street to set up a separate convention for the Spokane delegation. She promptly appointed herself chairman.

Once back in Spokane, May created the Washington Political Equality League with headquarters in the Hutton Building. As president, she forged ahead, generously investing her money, energy, and time in the suffrage cause. She hosted dinners, wrote press releases for the newspapers, and hired a professional publicist to handle things while she maneuvered her nearly three-hundred-pound frame and booming voice around the state, making speeches and waving from parade floats.

Finally, in 1910, women's suffrage was approved in the state of Washington, first by the legislature, then by the voters. After the victory, the suffrage organizations dissolved, except for May's Washington Political Equality League, which reorganized into a nonpartisan group.

When she was appointed to the Spokane Charities Commission, May took to cruising around town in her snappy red Thomas Flyer, attacking institutions and suggesting courses of corrective action. When she reported her findings directly to the press, City Hall was appalled. May didn't care; she had the money and political clout to get things done, and despite her crass exterior, many of her political friends admired her wisdom and courage.

Old-line Democrats who disliked Hutton needed the feminine votes she had so forcefully championed, and appointed her the first woman delegate to the 1912 Democratic National Convention in Baltimore. Al's only advice to his wife before she left was "just don't made an unholy show of yourself." When she returned from the convention totally burned-out from politics, Al presented May with a new building project, a spacious hilltop mansion. May focused her energies into decorating, and two years later the Huttons moved into their elegant new home, which featured stately pillars, terraces, and mountain views.

May was now in her fifties, her health failing from the diabetes her doctors had diagnosed years earlier. Although she had been advised to change her diet, May ignored the advice and continued to satisfy her large appetite for rich foods. When she began to suffer the effects of the disease and finally decided to heed her doctors' advice, it was too late.

May's health was declining rapidly when rumors of World War I began swirling in the distance. Unable to resist getting involved in the crusade for peace but too weak to launch a vigorous campaign, May sponsored theatrical productions and hosted a reception for the Washington State Federation of Women's Clubs on the lawn of her elegant mansion. Attended by more than one thousand friends and delegates, May presided over the festivities from her wheelchair and proudly signed a petition of Women for Peace to be presented to President Woodrow Wilson.

It was the last public appearance for May Arkwright Hutton, who died in 1915 at the age of fifty-five. Her obituary appeared in newspapers across the country and was carried on national wire services.

Big, bold May Hutton began her Western adventure as a miners' cook and died a millionaire. A fearless champion of the underdog, a political reformer, and a philanthropist, May Arkwright Hutton was a truly liberated woman.

MARY HUNTER AUSTIN

[*1868–1934*]

For all the toll the desert takes of a man
it gives compensations, deep breaths, deep sleep,
and the communion of the stars ... It is hard
to escape the sense of mastery
as the stars move in the wide clear heavens
to risings and settings unobscured.

—Mary Hunter Austin, *The Land of Little Rain*

"MARY, MARY, please try to keep up with the wagon. We have many miles left to cover and you are not helping the matter by going off by yourself!" Mary's exasperated mother shouted at her nineteen-year-old daughter, who had ridden off again into the desert. She could not understand for the life of her why Mary had to ride a horse when she could have ridden with the family in the wagon.

As if in a daze, Mary turned in the direction of her mother's words and was astonished at how far she had ridden into this unusual land. She was utterly fascinated by the dry, hostile desert that surrounded her, a land so different from the soft, green hills of Illinois. She marveled at the ability of shrubs and plants to survive in the harsh environment, and she was eager to explore the canyons and dry creek beds. But that would have to wait. Mary dug her heels into her horse's flanks and galloped toward the rumbling wagon.

The spell of the desert Southwest would seduce many writers, but few have expressed it more poignantly than Mary Hunter Austin. This prolific writer would author thirty books, hundreds of articles, essays, poems, and plays that glorified nature and native people in the wilds of the West.

MARY HUNTER AUSTIN *authored thirty books. Courtesy The*
Huntington Library, San Marino, California.

A pioneer author in the nature-writing of the Southwest, Austin is considered the interpreter of the southwestern region during the first third of the twentieth century. Her work would one day be compared to that of Ralph Waldo Emerson, Henry Thoreau, and John Muir, a fitting tribute for Austin, who spent many of her happiest moments in the company of the great literary stars of the early twentieth century.

Although Austin produced a huge volume of works and was a celebrated writer in her day, she was impossible to categorize. A mystic, a naturalist, and a feminist and student of Indian culture, Mary Austin wrote everything: novels, poems, essays, articles, science fiction, and plays.

Mary Hunter Austin was born in 1868 in Carlinville in the prairie country of southwestern Illinois. Her father, George Hunter, a country lawyer, had emigrated from England and served in the Union Army at the outbreak of the Civil War in 1861. His poor health and repeated malarial fevers led to his discharge three years later.

Mary was the fourth child to arrive to the semi-invalid, loving father and a withdrawn, disapproving mother. Her younger sister, Jennie, the sibling Mary shared affection and companionship with during her first ten years, died during childhood from diphtheria that she had contracted from Mary.

Mary believed that a pattern ran under her life and that it rose to the surface during her creative years. When she was five years old, Mary was struck with the realization that she also possessed another inner, richer personality that she named the "I-Mary." She referred to this inner self as the In-knower or sometimes the Genius, clarifying that, "I am not a genius, but within me there dwells a Genius that creates." She would claim later that this interior I-Mary wrote many of her best works in a state of virtual trance, hardly aware of what she was doing.

When Mary's adored father died in October 1878, followed by the death of her sister Jennie a few months later, Mary became lonely and withdrawn. She received little understanding or comfort from her mother, who ignored her and gave what little affection she had to the third child, the son she relied on to become the family's support when he grew up. Meanwhile, the family managed as best they could on the sparse inheritance left by George Hunter.

When she was sixteen, Mary enrolled in small Blackburn College, in her hometown, where she majored in science, astonishing her mother. "English I can study by myself, for science I have to have laboratories and a teacher," explained Mary. She graduated after packing a four-year college education into two and a half years, earning a bachelor of science degree in 1888. Her intense, driven nature would occasionally produce a nervous breakdown, the first of which took place during her college years. A year after graduation, she moved

In 1891, twenty-three-year-old MARY *married* STAFFORD WALLACE AUSTIN, *an irrigation engineer.*
Courtesy The Huntington Library, San Marino, California.

with her family to the desert on the edge of the San Joaquin Valley in southern
California, the site of her brother's homestead claim.

The family traveled westward by train, passing vast, open stretches of desert
that Mary found brooding and aloof. She would form a different opinion of San
Francisco, where the family stopped to visit with relatives. While exploring the
city with a cousin, Mary became enchanted with the city's beauty and sophisti-
cation and dreamed of returning. To reach their destination in Tejon, the family
had to travel to a point a hundred miles north from Los Angeles, a journey that
Mary completed on horseback while her family rode in a wagon.

Once the family was settled, Mary explored her surroundings on her horse,
noting the climate and seasons, talking with sheepherders, Indians, and Spanish-
speaking cowboys. She studied cattle and coyotes, attended round-ups and
brandings, and learned how Indians lived off the land. She later came to know
intimately and love this triangular portion of southeastern California that extends
from the eastern slopes of the Sierra Nevada and Nevada border south to the
Mojave Desert, the area Mary called "the land of little rain."

Before long, Mary was ready to strike out on her own and found a job as a
schoolteacher in a small community on the fringes of the desert. She continued

teaching and exploring the land until 1891, when twenty-three-year-old Mary married Stafford Wallace Austin, an irrigation engineer. For several years the couple would relocate to various towns in the remote Owens Valley of eastern California, where her husband attempted to start his own business. Mary began writing about the lonely, surrounding desert and the native inhabitants that impressed her so intensely, and found a market for her work in a few regional magazines.

Wallace Austin's attempts at starting a business failed, so he accepted a position of schoolteacher, and later became the Inyo County superintendent of schools. When the Austins moved to the town of Independence, Mary was enchanted by the area's stark, arid beauty, the mountains of the Sierra Nevada, and desolate Death Valley. The dramatic scenery of the Owens Valley would become a fountain of creativity and spiritual strength for Mary, one she would nurture long after she left the area.

After the birth of her only child, Ruth, a severely retarded daughter who was later institutionalized, the Austin marriage began to crumble. Many separations followed in the next several years, with divorce finally occurring in 1914. Mary's other tenuous relationship, the one with her disapproving mother, fared no better. The differences that divided Mary and her mother were never reconciled before the death of Mrs. Hunter, an event that left Mary grief stricken.

In her determination to establish a literary identity, Mary became consumed with her surroundings, studying with intensity the desert's native plants and creatures, including the Native Americans who lived there. She wrote about their value and beauty and celebrated the untamed, rugged land in articles that she sold to Western magazines. Her involvement with the Paiute tribe led to a life-long respect for their traditions and a lifelong crusade for their rights. Attracted to their beliefs and mystical traditions, Austin adapted some of their techniques to enhance her own creative powers.

However, the combination of trying to raise a retarded daughter while teaching school and writing became an overwhelming burden for Mary and led to a nervous breakdown in 1898. For treatment, she went to a hospital in San Francisco, where she attended a lecture by the philosopher William James. Impressed by James's intellectual powers and their conversations about creativity and consciousness that followed, Mary was inspired to return home and resume her writing life.

A year later Mary packed up her daughter and returned to San Francisco, where she hoped to find medical help for Ruth's retardation. While in the area, she also planned on visiting with Charles Lummis, an eccentric magazine editor and scholar of Indian folklore and Spanish art. Lummis would become a friend and valuable resource for Mary, as a publisher for her work and advisor and mentor. But more importantly, he introduced Mary to his literary circle, many members of whom became Mary's lifelong friends. Stimulated by these intellectual, creative people, Mary was filled with inspiration to write again. She took Ruth back home to Independence, where Wallace was waiting.

Mary began writing in earnest about the land she had come to love in a series of fourteen essays that eventually became *The Land of Little Rain*, published in 1903. Her passionate prose was well received by critics and readers, who were fascinated by her accounts of Indian life and her descriptions of the haunting landscape. Mary went on to write a collection of stories, *The Basket Woman;* a romantic novel, *Isidro*; and a collection of regional sketches, *The Flock*.

After the success of her first book, Mary felt a closer kinship with her literary friends in the Bay Area, a situation that left her both restless and resentful of her desert isolation. She reached out to her friends in San Francisco and accepted their invitations to visit. During her stays she was introduced to more of the city's writers and artists and added them to her circle of friends. She also explored the charming and rugged coast of the Monterey Peninsula and Carmel, where a colony of artists and writers was emerging.

Once the decision had been made to institutionalize Ruth in a Santa Clara facility, Mary decided to leave Wallace and the Valley she had once cherished for the bohemian life in the coastal village of Carmel. When Mary arrived at Carmel, she was thirty-eight years old, a rugged, self-reliant, and unconventional woman with a stout body, high forehead, prominent jaw, and a head full of red-gold hair.

With money from her successful first book, she built a house in Carmel in 1907 and became a member of the artists' colony there, a group that included the poet George Sterling, novelist Jack London, and Ambrose Bierce. Because her attachment to the coastal area did not have the same depth as her former desert landscape, Austin's main stimulus was her group of eccentric artistic friends, who met at the end of the day and conversed the evening away.

When she was forty years old, Austin was stunned by the news that she had terminal breast cancer with less than a year to live. Refusing to follow her doctor's recommendation for a mastectomy, Austin chose to keep her illness a secret from her friends in Carmel and decided to spend what time she had left traveling abroad. During a visit in Italy she learned of a Catholic convent near Rome where total immersion in the act of prayer was practiced. After completing a retreat there, Austin's pain and tumor had disappeared and never returned.

Austin traveled on to Paris and London, where she met many artistic and literary contemporaries she admired, William Butler Yeats, H. G. Wells, Henry James, and Joseph Conrad. Yeats and Wells were impressed by Mary and referred to her as "the most intelligent American woman they had ever met." In London, she stayed at the home of Herbert Hoover and was introduced to Hilaire Belloc. After a three-year sojourn in Europe, Austin was packed and ready to set sail for New York.

After settling into an apartment in New York City, Austin began preparing her play *The Arrow Maker* for the stage. She continued to meet new friends, journalists Lincoln Steffens and Ida Tarbell, Margaret Sanger, and labor leader Elizabeth Gurley Flynn. Through the quarter-century of her life that still remained, Austin continued to write and lecture on the rights of women and Native Americans, and on her theories of the origins and structure of poetry. Eventually she authored thirty books, usually one a year, and more than 250 articles, poetry, and several plays. After a time, letters from her friends back in Carmel would draw her back to the West Coast.

The property Austin had purchased in Carmel years earlier sat under towering pines and old oaks, offering privacy and a peek of the sea, the perfect setting for the small cottage she had built on it. After moving into her new home, where she lived the simple life, Mary began work on another play. Several months later, she returned to New York, hoping to reinforce her income by establishing new contacts for her work.

Austin wrote more plays and books in New York and found new publishers and producers for her work. She also added Fannie Hurst, Willa Cather, Sinclair Lewis, and George Bernard Shaw to her circle of friends. While she was in New York, her divorce from Wallace became final, a few years before the United States announced its involvement in the War in Europe in 1917. Needing a change of scenery, Austin accepted an invitation to be a guest at the house of a friend who had settled near Santa Fe, New Mexico.

The view from seven thousand feet on the western flank of the Sangre de Cristo Mountains near Sante Fe brought back memories of the Owens Valley, and provided Austin with feelings of having returned home. Everything about the area enchanted her, the dramatic play of light, the sweeping landscape, towering mountains, and blazing sunsets. In this stimulating atmosphere Austin lavished her energies on community affairs and cultural activities, while her work and her health faltered.

On the verge of nervous collapse, Austin hired a car and fled to Taos and the home of a friend, where she found the peace and quiet to finish her novel *No. 26 Jayne Street*. Afterward, she arranged a trip to Tucson, Arizona, where she explored remote Indian villages, which brought back the familiar tug of excitement to create another series of prose sketches, like the ones she wrote for *The*

Land of Little Rain. After extensive research and more than two thousand miles of travel in the Southwest, Austin began writing *The Land of Journey's Ending*.

Austin returned to Santa Fe for good in 1924, the same year *The Land of Journey's Ending* was published. She had a simple adobe home built in a budding artists' colony above the town, a community of walled gardens, flat-roofed adobe houses, and a central plaza. Austin called her house Casa Querida (The Beloved House), and her writing was soon infused with new energy. She became involved with the preservation of Native American arts and the American Indian Defense Association. Her concern for Colorado River water resources prompted her to speak out against and write articles condemning the proposed Boulder Dam.

Austin became a close friend of photographer Ansel Adams, with whom she collaborated on the book *Taos Pueblo*. Adams and his wife remained close and loyal to Austin until her death, taking her somewhat difficult personality in stride. After Austin's death, Adams wrote, "Seldom have I met and known anyone of such intellectual and spiritual power and discipline."

Toward the end of her life, as her health was failing, Austin contracted to write her autobiography, an assignment that would cause her much anxiety. But she completed the book, *Earth Horizon*, in 1930, two years before it was published. This last work of Austin appealed to a greater audience than her earlier works, due to its designation as a Literary Guild book club selection.

On August 13, 1934, Mary Hunter Austin died in her sleep at her beloved home, a few weeks before her sixty-sixth birthday. Her ashes were placed in a rock crypt at the top of Picacho Peak in the Sangre de Cristo Mountains, overlooking Santa Fe from an elevation of ten thousand feet.

Because Mary Hunter Austin created such a wide variety of works in so many different fields, critics found her difficult to categorize. Was she a novelist, poet, playwright, essayist, naturalist, or feminist? Hence her novels, poetry, plays, nature essays, and studies of Indian culture and feminism would sink into obscurity for nearly half a century after her death. Toward the end of the twentieth century, however, Austin's works experienced a rebirth, earning her celebrated work, *The Land of Little Rain*, praise as a classic of Western American nature writing.

MARY JANE ELIZABETH COLTER

[*1869–1958*]

This talented, Stetson-wearing architect
achieved her dreams and a high degree of creative power
before most women had the right to vote.
Colter's influence lingers across the Southwest today,
along with the haunting structures she created
using materials of the earth,
colors of the desert, and Native American designs.

PETITE WOMAN IN TROUSERS and a tall Stetson hat stood on the edge of a rocky precipice in the morning sun, watching as the great, ancient canyon came alive in endless ribbons of color. Awed by the spectacular beauty of the canyon, she thought of the ancient inhabitants who occupied this region, living in harmony in structures made from the earth.

Early morning was Mary Colter's favorite time of day, and as usual, she was at the building site well before the construction crew, following a pattern she had set for herself many years ago when working on her first architectural job for the Fred Harvey Company. A perfectionist, she liked to arrive early to examine the placement of every stone in the project before "the boys" arrived. She stopped in front of a boulder that she realized had been placed incorrectly into a wall. Appalled, Colter determined that the whole section would have to be dismantled and completely rebuilt. She lit another cigarette and waited for the crew.

Few women carved their name into the Southwestern landscape as creatively as did Mary Jane Colter. During her forty-six-year association with the Fred Harvey Company, this talented and prolific architect and interior decorator

Few women carved their name into the Southwestern landscape as creatively as did
MARY JANE ELIZABETH COLTER. *Courtesy Grand Canyon National Park Museum Collection.*

would create a collection of distinctive structures along the Santa Fe Railway, a line that stretched from Los Angeles to Chicago. Through her work, Colter introduced the Southwest's unique Native American architecture, arts, and crafts to the rest of the country during the early twentieth century. Her influence still lingers across the Southwest today, and is most evident on the south rim of the Grand Canyon. This dramatic natural site in Northern Arizona remains the showcase for Colter's work. It is where the largest collection of her structures still stands, including five that have been designated National Historic Landmarks.

The fact that Colter was able to achieve her dreams and wield a high degree of creative power at a time when most women did not have the right to vote says much about her talent and character. Though she was a woman working in a man's world, Colter's innate sense of style, vivid imagination, and strong personality enabled her to make her mark in history.

Mary Jane Elizabeth Colter was born in 1869 in Pittsburgh, Pennsylvania, far from the southwestern region that held such fascination for her. Her parents moved often during Mary's childhood, finally settling in St. Paul, Minnesota, when Mary was eleven. It was in St. Paul that Colter became aware of the city's large Sioux Indian population and developed an interest in Indian art and culture. One of her most cherished possessions was a collection of Plains Indians drawings, which her mother threatened to destroy during a smallpox outbreak. Mary hid the drawings from her mother and kept them for the rest of her life.

While in school, Colter excelled in art classes and dreamed of attending an art institute someday to learn how to design and decorate buildings. Her father opposed the idea, but after his death in 1886, the persistent seventeen-year-old Colter convinced her mother to send her to San Francisco's California School of Design so she could someday help support the family.

As a student and architect's assistant in San Francisco, Colter learned the mechanics of designing buildings and witnessed changes taking place in Western architecture. In 1890, the year she graduated, the era of European-influenced architecture was being replaced by the revival of early Spanish California mission design, a style considered more suitable for the Western region.

As she had promised her mother, Colter returned to St. Paul, where she accepted a job teaching mechanical drawing to high school students. During her fifteen years as a teacher, Colter also became active in the city's art circles, studied archaeology, lectured on art and history, and wrote book reviews.

In 1900, while vacationing in San Francisco, Colter designed an elaborate display of Indian baskets for a private home. When an executive with the Fred Harvey Company saw the display, he told Colter about his company's new project, designing showcases for Indian crafts. Ready for a career change, Colter submitted

COLTER *decorated the Indian Building at the Alvarado Hotel in Albuquerque, New Mexico. Courtesy Grand Canyon National Park Museum Collection.*

an application to the Fred Harvey Company's headquarters in Kansas City and was hired a year later.

The Fred Harvey Company had been operating hotels, restaurants, shops, and dining cars for the Atchison, Topeka, and Santa Fe Railway since 1876. Harvey Houses—clean, moderately priced establishments where passengers could dine, shop, and rest—were located at stops along the twelve thousand miles of railway. Known as the "civilizer of the West," the Fred Harvey Company maintained high standards and provided gracious service by prim, proper Harvey Girls in starched black and white uniforms.

In the early 1900s, interest in train travel to the Southwest began to rise, a situation that prompted the Fred Harvey Company and the Santa Fe Railway to feature train depots and tourist attractions in Native American and California Mission Revival style. Colter was given the job of decorating the Indian Building at the Alvarado Hotel in Albuquerque, New Mexico.

A longtime fascination with Native American culture and art enabled Colter to create a stunning display of the Fred Harvey Company's archaeological collection. She also featured native Navajo women in colorful tribal dress, weaving rugs and blankets on their looms, and Navajo silversmiths making their stunning

Hopi House interior, located on the south rim directly across from the El Tovar Hotel at the Grand Canyon. Courtesy Grand Canyon National Park Museum Collection.

silver jewelry. When the building opened in 1902 to an admiring crowd, Colter's forty-six-year association with the company was launched. But the company had no more work to offer at the time, forcing Colter to return to her teaching position in St. Paul. She would wait for three years before hearing from the Fred Harvey Company again.

In 1904 the Fred Harvey Company and the railroad began construction on El Tovar Hotel, a handsome luxury hotel on the south rim of the Grand Canyon. Colter's background in architecture and archaeology and her familiarity with Spanish-Indian culture made her a perfect candidate to decorate the new hotel's Indian gift shop. This assignment was the first in a body of work at the Canyon that eventually included eight structures and an inner-canyon ranch. It also raised Colter's status from that of interior decorator to designing architect.

After Colter's first two decorating assignments, she was hired to design a gift shop to resemble a native Hopi dwelling. It was to be named Hopi House and located on the south rim directly across from El Tovar Hotel. Colter enlisted the aid of a scholar of Hopi culture and Hopi laborers and designed a simple, flat-roofed Pueblo-style structure of rustic native stone and wood similar to Oraibi, a Hopi pueblo dating to the 1100s. Built on several levels, Hopi House featured a primitive interior with thick walls and cement floors designed to look like mud. In rooms decorated with authentic Native American art and crafts, Colter featured native Hopi weavers, basket makers, artists, and potters.

In 1910, the forty-one-year-old Colter was working full time for the Fred Harvey Company, designing and decorating hotels, restaurants, and Union Station facilities. During her career, she decorated everything from hotels and dining cars to company china and employee uniforms. For a woman to hold a position with such power in a large company was a rarity in this period of American history. Even more challenging was the fact that Colter worked for two bosses, the Fred Harvey Company and the Santa Fe Railway, parties who often disagreed. Although she kept an apartment and office in Kansas City, headquarters of the Fred Harvey Company, Colter was rarely home. She led a nomad's life, usually working somewhere along the line, staying at Harvey hotels, designing and supervising construction on new building projects or remodeling and redecorating others.

Considering the number of her creations, Colter was undoubtedly quite effective at defending her views. It is hardly surprising to learn that she was considered unreasonable and uncompromising by some of the men who worked for her. As a lone woman executive, she spent a lifetime championing her aesthetic vision, a habit that may have led to the imperious attitude she is said to have developed in her later life.

A petite woman, five feet one inch, with bright violet-blue eyes and flyaway hair, Colter liked to chain smoke and wear Stetson hats. A perfectionist and workaholic, she was known to be outspoken, demanding, and driven. She often arrived at a job site early in the morning and stayed late in the day, scrutinizing the placement of every stone. One day during construction at the Grand Canyon, workers placed a large stone in the wrong place. When Colter noticed the error, she insisted the section be dismantled and completely rebuilt.

In 1914 the Fred Harvey Company constructed an eight-mile road along the Grand Canyon's south rim for sightseeing tours. They called on Colter to design a rest stop at the end of the road, where visitors could stretch their legs, view the Canyon, and enjoy the company-provided tea and wafers. Guided by her fascination for rustic beginnings, Colter wanted to create a structure that appeared indigenous to the setting, one that blended into the natural, rugged landscape without detracting from it. The result was a rough, rustic home of natural timber and boulders, suitable for a hermit. Perched on the edge of a cliff, Hermit's Rest blended into the landscape so unassumingly that members of the construction crew made comments about its ancient appearance. When the comments reached Colter, she laughed, saying, "You can't imagine what it cost to make it look this old."

Colter's other structures on the Grand Canyon's south rim also followed her philosophy of creating buildings of indigenous materials and methods. When she designed Lookout Studio, she used limestone and logs to resemble the ancient ruins of the region, then added terraces to allow visitors to move in and out of the building and enjoy the awesome rim views. When it was finished, the structure looked as if it had sprouted from its surroundings.

In 1917, at the start of World War I, train travel was beginning to wane, so all expansion plans were put on hold. Three years later, when the war was over, trains were again rolling across the Southwest with carloads of passengers bound for the Grand Canyon. The newest Fred Harvey Company attraction was mule trips for visitors eager to explore the inner canyon via an eight-mile trek down the Kaibab Trail to the canyon's bottom. It was also the site of Colter's next assignment.

Colter was fifty-three years old when she created Phantom Ranch to accommodate weary guests at the floor of the Canyon. Using stones from Phantom Creek and other Canyon materials, Colter constructed a cluster of modest cottages with a dining hall and recreational building. Supplies, as well as the architect, had to be transported to the site by mule, an arduous journey that descends through one mile of elevation. When Phantom Ranch opened with accommodations for seventy-five in 1922, it blended into the landscape so well, a whole new building style was born. Known as National Park Service Rustic, the simple design of Phantom Ranch would be used as a model and promoted by the National Park Service to architects at other parks.

Colter's next assignment, in the following year, took her away from the Canyon to Gallup, New Mexico, to design and decorate the new El Navajo Hotel. This modern building, which featured long, low arches, horizontal and vertical window groupings, and projecting balconies, was a bold move for the Fred Harvey Company and the Santa Fe Railway. Their plan was to combine modern architecture with ancient art and to feature unprecedented Native American artwork. They relied on Colter's good relations with Indian artists, which allowed her to decorate the hotel with authentic reproductions of the sacred sand paintings used in Navajo religious rituals, and to arrange an impressive Navajo blessing ceremony for the hotel's opening day in 1923.

Later that year, the Santa Fe Railway acquired La Fonda, a romantic inn located in downtown Santa Fe, and Colter was assigned to decorate its interior. The newly expanded 156-room hotel presented an enormous challenge to Colter,

The Watchtower, a remarkable 70-foot structure perched at the highest point on the south rim of the Grand Canyon. Courtesy Grand Canyon National Park Museum Collection.

who had been injured in an automobile accident before the assignment and had to supervise the entire project in a wheelchair.

In 1930, the Fred Harvey Company and the railway erected their last resort hotel in the eastern Arizona town of Winslow. Located within visiting distance of the Painted Desert, Petrified Forest, and Hopi pueblos, the site was a perfect setting for Colter's work. She designed La Posada, a rambling structure set on eight acres of land, to resemble the hacienda of a wealthy Spanish don. She spared no expense creating the handsome Spanish Mediterranean–style building with seventy rooms and five suites. A furniture factory was installed on the site to produce the "antique" furniture Colter required, and her meticulous attention to detail appeared throughout the building. The structure's exterior was painted a soft pink to match the color of the earth beneath it, and the building was surrounded with acres of orchards and gardens with hidden shrines and fountains. La Posada was Colter's favorite project.

Colter was in her sixties in 1932 when she was summoned back to the Grand Canyon to design two more structures, a combination observation building and rest stop, and a hotel for the budget minded. As in her earlier designs, Colter envisioned rustic structures to compliment the Canyon's natural beauty.

This time, before beginning the project, Colter toured Native American ruins in airplanes and automobiles, where she took photographs, made drawings, and studied the techniques of the ancient Anasazi, or Hisatsinom. The result was the Watchtower, a remarkable seventy-foot structure perched at the highest point on the south rim. Built of rough stone and modeled after the ancient towers at some Southwestern ruins, the building featured authentic rock carvings and looked as old as the land it stood upon. Colter was so excited about this project that she wrote a hundred-page handbook about the structure's history for guides of the Harvey tours. News of the Watchtower's opening in 1932 was featured on radio and in hundreds of newspapers throughout the country.

To satisfy the visitors to the Canyon who sought more affordable accommodations than those offered at the luxurious El Tovar, the Fred Harvey Company decided to build another hotel, Bright Angel Lodge. Colter was named architect and designed a comfortable, rustic lodge made of logs and stone with individual cabins and a main building that housed shops, restaurants, and an extraordinary fireplace with tiers of Canyon rock layered in order of geological formation. The Bright Angel took two years to build, at a cost of $500,000, and opened in 1935 with a barbecue attended by two thousand people.

Colter spent the next several years working at various Fred Harvey Company decorating projects along the Santa Fe line. She decorated diners on the railway's new Super Chief train, supervised renovation of Union Station in Kansas City, and returned to the Grand Canyon to oversee construction of two dormitories for Fred Harvey Company employees. In 1939, when the new $11 million Union Station in Los Angeles was completed, seventy-year-old Colter was on hand to install the Native American flavor that had been associated with the Santa Fe Railway for many years.

Colter went along when Fred Harvey Company moved its headquarters from Kansas City to Chicago in 1940. A few years later, the onset of World War II put a dent in the resort hotel business, and expansion programs were shelved. The company that once operated seventy-five Harvey Houses now operated fewer than half that number.

With no new buildings to design or decorate, Colter began thinking about retirement and traveled to New Mexico, where she indulged her passion for archaeology and Native American architecture at the Indian cliff dwellings at Mesa Verde National Park. Retirement had to wait, however, as the Fred Harvey Company needed Colter in 1947 to decorate the interior of their new acquisition near Holbrook, Arizona, the Painted Desert Inn, which had been built in 1938 by the Civilian Conservation Corps.

Colter prepared to retire completely in 1948, after having served the Fred Harvey Company for forty-six years. She moved to Santa Fe near the Indian pueblos and culture she loved. She also agreed to complete one more assignment for the company, the design and decoration of a new cocktail lounge at La Fonda in Sante Fe, the inn she had decorated years ago from a wheelchair.

After the final job was done, Colter officially retired and settled down in a small Spanish-Indian adobe home. She continued collecting the Indian jewelry she treasured for the rest of her life, and even designed some pieces herself. In 1957, when Colter heard that her favorite La Posada Inn was put up for sale due to declining railroad travel, she lamented, "There's such a thing as living too long." She died the following year in 1958 at eighty-nine years of age.

Although some of Colter's work no longer remains, the collection of haunting stone buildings on the south rim of the Grand Canyon keeps her memory alive. She never married or had a family, but her legacy lives on in the remarkable structures that continue Colter's celebration of the southwestern landscape and Native American art.

NELLIE TAYLOE ROSS

[1876–1977]

*This reluctant politician from Wyoming
proved that it's never too late for a woman
to change her mind or to toss her hat into the ring.
Nellie Ross was thrust into politics by her husband's death,
and went on to set records and open doors for women
on both state and national levels.*

O! NO! IT CAN'T BE TRUE! Her dear William, the man she married twenty-two years ago, the father of her sons, and the governor of Wyoming could not be dead. How could the pain in his stomach turn out to be a ruptured appendix? Oh, William, William, what will the boys and I do without you? What will the people of Wyoming do?

Nellie Tayloe Ross was still reeling from the shock of her husband's unexpected death when Democratic Party leaders asked Nellie if she would fill the remaining two years of her husband's term and accept the party's nomination for governor. There was no time to waste with a general election coming up in a few weeks, and a state law required that a successor be named. Nellie was astounded and wondered how they could even consider her a candidate for governor.

It was impossible! She had never considered a career in politics and had no political experience other than acting as confidant to her husband. In fact, Nellie had always believed that a woman's place was in the home, and for the past twenty-two years she had devoted herself to her home and family and her charitable work with women's clubs. How could the Democratic Party even think she could handle the responsibilities required of a governor? She thought about her

---

NELLIE TAYLOE ROSS *always believed a woman's place was in the home, until her husband's death, when she was asked to be a candidate for governor. Courtesy Wyoming Division of Cultural Resources.*

WILLIAM B. ROSS, NELLIE'S *husband, died unexpectedly while serving as governor of Wyoming. Courtesy Wyoming Division of Cultural Resources.*

husband and of his policies and plans for the second half of his term. Who would uphold his fine ideals? Nellie felt confused and needed time to think.

Democratic Party leaders, in the meantime, were anxious to name a successor and candidate and interpreted Nellie's silence as agreement. They nominated her for governor of Wyoming.

For a woman who once believed her place was on the domestic front, Nellie Tayloe Ross proceeded to amass a record of achievements in the political world that would take her far from her comfortable home. This reluctant politician was thrust unexpectedly into the highest elected office in her state, where she abandoned her conventional life in Cheyenne society and established a series of firsts for women in the state of Wyoming and in the nation.

Nellie Davis Tayloe was born on November 29, 1876, in St. Joseph, Missouri, into a prominent Southern family. A frail child, Nellie was educated in private schools and moved with her family to Omaha, Nebraska, where she completed a kindergarten teaching program and taught school.

A few years later, in 1902, Nellie married a young lawyer, William Bradford Ross, and moved with him to Cheyenne, Wyoming. After establishing a successful general law practice, William Ross occasionally ran for political office. Unfortunately, he was a Democrat in a Republican state and often lost. But finally, in 1922, twenty years after his arrival in Wyoming, William Ross was elected governor.

Nellie Tayloe Ross devoted the first twenty years of her marriage to her duties as wife and mother of four sons, one of whom died in childhood. Although she was an intelligent, educated woman living in a state where women had been granted the vote back in 1869, Nellie was not interested in the pursuit of politics. She did, however, strongly support her husband's policies, often assisting him with his political works.

In October 1924, less than two years after his election as governor, Nellie's husband died unexpectedly from complications following surgery. With a general election scheduled a few weeks after William Ross's death, and state law requiring that a successor be named immediately, Democratic Party leaders asked Nellie Tayloe Ross to fill the remaining two years of her husband's term and accept the party's nomination for governor.

Still grief-stricken over the death of her husband, and with little political experience, Nellie needed time to think and did not reply immediately. With her silence interpreted as compliance, Nellie Tayloe Ross was nominated for governor on October 14.

Nellie accepted the nomination with the understanding that she would continue to support her husband's programs, which she believed in and understood better than anyone. She also needed a purpose in her life to help relieve the grief of widowhood.

Nellie's opponent was the Republican nominee, Eugene J. Sullivan of Casper, an attorney with ties to the oil industry. At the time, the state and the nation were immersed in the Teapot Dome scandal, which involved federal oil lands, some of which were located in Wyoming, and Sullivan's ties would not help his campaign.

Rather than organize a campaign for election, Nellie simply stated her intentions in two open letters, while her friends sponsored a few political advertisements. Nellie did not need to do more because she already had two main advantages in this election; she had the voters' sympathy for her widowhood, and she was a woman in a state that took pride in being first.

Although Nellie had not actively participated in the women's suffrage campaign in Wyoming, she was well aware that she lived in the first state to grant voting rights to women. Nellie claimed that a vote for her was a tribute to her husband, and she may have been right. But this particular election also provided Wyoming with an opportunity to be the first state to elect a woman governor. Even if Texas elected Miriam Ferguson, wife of an impeached former governor in their November election, Wyoming's inaugural date was held earlier than the one in Texas.

Nellie Ross won the election easily, even though other Democrats in Wyoming and throughout the country did not fare well that year. On January 5, 1925, less than three months after her husband's death, Nellie Tayloe Ross became the thirteenth governor of Wyoming, and the first woman to hold that position in the state or in the nation. When she was sworn in, the new governor of Wyoming was still dressed in mourning clothes. Nellie Ross became the state and country's first woman governor by a narrow margin, a mere sixteen days before the inauguration of Miriam Ferguson in Texas.

During her inaugural address, Governor Nellie Ross briefly stated that her administration would be a continuation of her husband's. Later, in her first major speech, she called for reductions in state spending and taxes, for state assistance to the agricultural industry, and for banking reform. She also supported protective legislation for miners, women, and children, and asked for state ratification of the federal amendment prohibiting child labor.

With a legislature dominated by Republicans, Ross realized that she would receive little cooperation. Sometimes she was able to work out compromises; other times she exercised her power of the veto. She weeded out those in her administration who were not meeting her expectations, and she advocated improved law enforcement for Prohibition. She also challenged the federal government on issues of federal lands and water allocation

Ross felt the pressure of the public eye on her actions, knowing that any error she made as governor might reflect poorly on women everywhere who were interested in pursuing elective office. She was aware of her fishbowl existence, of being an object of curiosity to those who hounded her office and her front porch, so she declined invitations to speak all over the country.

When she finally did make an appearance, like the one in President Calvin Coolidge's inaugural parade in Washington, D.C., she received an overwhelming ovation. Many Easterners still considered Wyoming part of the wild, uncivilized

Wyoming State Capitol building, 1930. Courtesy Wyoming Division of Cultural Resources.

West, and its cultured, gracious governor created a sensation simply because she didn't fit their expectations.

The Democrats nominated Nellie Ross for reelection in 1926, hoping to convince women voters that a rejection of Ross would be a rejection of women's suffrage. The Republicans, on the other hand, were still smarting from Ross's veto of a special election bill and were suggesting that a man would be a better governor than a woman.

The bill that Ross exercised her veto power over was a bill requiring a special election (instead of appointment by the governor) to fill a vacancy in Wyoming's delegation to the U.S. Senate. The veto angered the Republicans, who feared the governor would appoint a fellow Democrat to fill the term of an elderly Republican senator who was not expected to survive his term.

This governor's unpopular veto is said to have caused her narrow 1926 loss to the Republican candidate, Frank C. Emerson. Others claimed that Ross was defeated simply because she was a Democrat in a Republican state, and the sympathy issue that had helped her in 1924 no longer applied.

After her term ended, Ross never ran for elective public office again, but she retained her interest in politics and remained in the public eye as an effective speaker and writer of magazine articles. A staunch Democrat, Ross became involved in national politics, serving as state committeewoman to the Democratic National Committee and later as its vice-chairman in charge of activities for women.

In 1928, she was on hand to second the presidential nomination of New York Governor Alfred E. Smith. With Eleanor Roosevelt, she headed the campaign drive launched by the party's Women's Division to generate support for Smith. Armed with her fame and fine speaking skills, Ross traveled around the country making endless speeches for Smith's election.

Four years later, Ross was actively involved in the Women's Speakers' Bureau, campaigning for the Democratic presidential nominee, Franklin D. Roosevelt. This time the Democratic candidate won, and when Roosevelt took office in 1932, he wanted to be the first president to appoint women to the cabinet. Aware of Ross's political savvy and devotion to the Democratic Party, the President considered Ross for several positions, finally appointing her director of the United States Mint, the first woman ever to hold the position.

Ross's job at the U.S. Mint involved American gold and silver bullion reserves and the minting of coins for the U.S. and several foreign governments. When she began her new job as director, she found a demoralized staff and meager budget, but Ross proved to be an effective administrator. She would be credited for automating the handling process for the gold and silver that flooded into U.S. government's coffers, and for reducing the costs of her operation by a significant margin. She managed to conquer problems of the Great Depression and World War II, and during her term introduced the Roosevelt dime, the Jefferson nickel, and the steel penny.

In 1950, Ross surprised the Congressional Appropriations Committee by reporting that she wanted to return about $1 million of her $4.8 million appropriation, a sum larger than she felt she needed. Ross also managed to reduce the labor needs of the mint by discharging nearly three thousand employees. Ross served as director of the Mint for four five-year terms, one of the few appointees to stay through Roosevelt's entire administration as well as that of Harry Truman.

Nellie Ross retired in 1953 after twenty years in Washington, when Dwight D. Eisenhower, a Republican, was elected President. She continued to live in Washington, D.C., lecturing, writing, and traveling. She died there in 1977 at the age of 101.

For a conventional woman who did not intend to have a political career, Nellie Tayloe Ross proved that it's never too late for a woman to change her mind or to toss her hat into the ring. Thrust into politics by her husband's death, she discovered a "second wind" that enabled her to set records on both state and national levels.

This reluctant politician became the first woman governor in Wyoming and in the United States, the first female director of the U.S. Mint, and the first woman to have her likeness imprinted on a medal made by the Mint. Nellie Tayloe Ross was also the first woman to be inscribed on the cornerstone of a government building, the Fort Knox gold depository, which had been built under her directorship.

JEANNETTE
PICKERING RANKIN

[1880–1973]

The country's first congresswoman,
a lifelong feminist and pacifist, created a furor across the nation
as the only member of Congress to vote against
declaring war on Japan after the bombing of Pearl Harbor.

T WAS THREE O'CLOCK in the morning on December 11, 1941, and the eyes and ears of her fellow congressmen were turned on her. Finally, the lone, weary woman in the chamber took a deep breath and announced, "No. I can't go to war and I refuse to send anyone else." With her vote, Jeannette Rankin from Montana, the nation's first U.S. Congresswoman, became the only member of either legislative body to vote against the country's entry into World War II after the bombing of Pearl Harbor.

The outrage her unpopular vote created could be heard across the country, and it began as soon as Rankin emerged from the House chamber. Confronted by an angry mob, she was chased into a telephone booth, from which she called the Capitol police to escort her back to her office. So unpopular was her vote that even her home state of Montana turned against her, forcing Rankin to complete her term as a "maverick Republican."

Having the country disagree with her pacifist beliefs was not the first time Jeannette Rankin had experienced public disapproval. Twenty-four years earlier, in 1917, during her first term as Congresswoman, Rankin voted against U.S. entry into World War I. Her strong isolationist stand would lose Rankin a seat in Congress and end her political career, but it never changed her quest for peace and women's rights.

JEANNETTE PICKERING RANKIN, *the nation's first congresswoman, often reminded girls about their opportunites. Courtesy Montana Historical Society.*

Jeannette Pickering Rankin was born in 1880 on a large ranch near Missoula, in the gun-toting and mining culture of Montana Territory. Her father had built a fortune in livestock, real estate, and mining, and her mother was a schoolteacher. As the eldest of seven children, Jeannette was expected to help care for her younger siblings. During her childhood she developed a strong bond with her only brother, Wellington, that lasted a lifetime. He became her biggest supporter and backed her in all of her ventures.

Jeannette's parents were sociable people who often had guests in their home. Their children grew into educated, well-rounded adults, comfortable with people from all walks of life. Jeannette enjoyed a close relationship with her father, who taught her how to run his business. He admired his eldest daughter's maturity and independent thinking and noted that in her youth Jeannette was decisive, a problem solver who seldom became ruffled.

Jeannette grew into a lovely, outspoken young woman with large gray eyes and lots of lustrous hair. Popular and outgoing, she enjoyed parties and dancing, but refused the many marriage proposals she received, preferring instead to establish a career without the responsibility of children.

Like many other educated pioneer women, Jeannette Rankin began her career as a schoolteacher after graduating from University of Montana in 1902. And like ambitious women before her, she soon became restless to move beyond the schoolhouse in rural Montana.

With her brother Wellington in law school at Harvard, Rankin went East to study social work at Harvard and the New York School of Philanthropy. In 1909 she began a career as a social worker in Seattle, Washington, where she joined the rising tide of sentiment for women's suffrage.

By 1910 she was lobbying for the cause in Washington, California, and Montana. A few years later, in 1914, she had become the legislative secretary of the National American Woman Suffrage Association and was leading a successful suffrage campaign in her native Montana. When a Montana legislator talked about introducing a bill for women's rights, Jeannette held him to the promise and went with him to speak before the House.

Rankin charmed the House with her total femininity, dispelling the idea that all suffragettes were middle aged and masculine. Although the bill missed by a narrow margin, Rankin was determined to achieve the vote for women of Montana. She campaigned across the territory like a whirlwind, with her well-organized followers working by her side, distributing literature, visiting small farms, and speaking on street corners, something that raised considerable eyebrows. But with Rankin in the lead, no one could keep her down.

In 1914, women were granted suffrage in Montana, six years before all American women could vote. The approval of suffrage in her state created an opportunity for Rankin to run for public office and launch her illustrious career. When asked about her state's passage of the suffrage bill, Rankin said, "men in the West had experienced pioneer conditions, so they gave women the vote, and then women decided to use it to improve things."

Rankin believed that now that the women in her state had the vote, they needed to gain the power to use it. She set her sights for a seat in the U.S. House of Representatives, winning the Republican primary for the nomination in 1916. With brother Wellington serving as campaign manager, Rankin ran as a Progressive Republican with the slogan "Preparedness will make for Peace." Stressing national suffrage, child welfare, Prohibition, tariff reform, and U.S. isolationism, Rankin won Montana's general election in November 1916, becoming the first Congresswoman in the United States.

As the first woman to hold a seat in either chamber, Rankin became a darling of the media and was showered with national attention. Rankin's swearing in could only be overshadowed by something as dramatic as war, a situation President Wilson was contemplating the evening Congress convened in April 1917.

From her years growing up in turbulent Montana Territory, Rankin had heard tales of violence, and she yearned for peace without lawlessness. Now, four days after taking her hard-fought seat in Congress, she faced a debate about whether the United States should declare war against Germany.

With the majority of women in the country still struggling for suffrage, Rankin was well aware that her vote spoke for all women, many of whom feared that a vote against war branded suffragists as unpatriotic. But the free-thinking daughter of the West, who had carried the banner of peace to Washington, D.C., now had to vote for or against entering World War I.

When her turn came to vote Rankin said, "I want to stand by my country and I cannot vote for war. I vote no." Not only did she cast a dissenting vote, she shattered a 140-year-old precedent by adding remarks on her vote during roll call. Although forty-eight other members of Congress also voted against the war, she was the only woman to have done so, and the press attacked her.

She was called everything from a dagger in the hands of the German propagandists, a dupe of the Kaiser, a member of the Hun army, to a crying schoolgirl. The *New York Times* would say that her vote against war provided "almost final proof of the feminine incapacity for straight reasoning." She was called a disgrace to womanhood, with her behavior proving how inadequate women were for the demands of public office. The suffragists denounced her with charges that she had betrayed them.

But the courageous Congresswoman from Montana remained cool under attack and moved on to other important matters. She fulfilled her duties as a representative by exposing deplorable working conditions at the U.S. Bureau of Printing and Engraving, which resulted in reforms. She championed the fight against blacklisting used by mining companies to discourage union organizing, and she introduced the first bill to allow women citizenship independent of their husbands.

As her first term as a Congresswoman drew to a close, Rankin campaigned for a seat in the Senate, but lost in the Republican primary. She then ran as a third-party candidate on the Nationalist Party ticket. But with the country in the midst of war and most women still fighting for suffrage, Rankin's refusal to pretend she was anything other than a committed pacifist proved to be her demise. Her former allies from the suffrage and temperance movements, still wanting to avoid being tainted by her antiwar views, called her a "colossal failure" and endorsed her opponent. With Rankin losing by a wide margin, her political career seemed over.

After the suffrage amendment was ratified in 1920 and all women in America could vote, Rankin spent the next sixteen years working for women's and children's issues and the Women's Peace Movement. She returned to the West and social work in Seattle, Washington. She traveled extensively, attending the Congress of the International Council of Women, and became an organizer for the National Council for the Prevention of War. She threw herself feverishly into the peace movement, working nonstop on one project after another. But by the late 1930s Rankin was convinced that war clouds were forming on the horizon.

In 1940 Rankin returned to Montana, where she maintained her legal residence, and announced her candidacy for the House seat she had vacated some twenty-two years earlier. With Wellington again at her side, she campaigned with the message, "Prepare to the limit for defense; keep our men out of Europe."

She took her campaign to the schools, where she told children about the threat of war and what could be done through the democratic process. She often reminded girls about their opportunities and said to the boys, "Someday one of you may be the husband of a President."

Rankin defeated her Democratic opponent on her antiwar platform in 1940 and returned to Congress, winning with a plurality of 9,264 votes. When she arrived back in Washington in January 1941, Rankin would not be met by all the hoopla that had marked her maiden appearance in Congress. Other women had

RANKIN *and suffragette* CARRIE CHAPMAN CATT *speaking from the balcony of the National American Woman Suffrage Association in 1917. Courtesy Montana Historical Society.*

followed in her footsteps, removing the novelty showered on pioneer women.

Back in office, Rankin rallied against resorting to armed force for any reason except an invasion of the continental U.S. Her belief was: "You can no more win a war than you can win an earthquake." But when the Japanese attacked Pearl Harbor on December 7, 1941, her words fell upon deaf ears.

Rankin was thrust once again into the position that so marked her first term in Congress twenty-two years earlier. Unable to get permission to address the House, the committed isolationist Rankin cast the only vote against entry into World War II. This time the public disapproval was more intense than before, but once the furor had died down, she finished her term by concentrating on humanitarian issues, such as aid for refugees. Her pacifist stance would deny her a seat in Congress in 1942 and bring an end to her political career. With no chance of reelection, Rankin left Washington and returned to Montana, where she kept a low profile caring for her elderly mother, occasionally visiting a cabin she owned in Georgia.

Once the war was over, Rankin began to travel extensively to Europe, Asia, Africa, and South America, continuing her study of the international peace movement. Ghandi's nonviolent activism held particular appeal for Rankin, and she made seven trips to India to study at Ghandi's ashram. During the 1950s she persistently questioned the United States' role in developing countries and opposed its involvement in Korea.

For twenty years Rankin lived in her cabin in Georgia, following the example of Thoreau and doing without electricity or running water. She opened camps and taught peace habits to children, preaching alternatives to the consumerist values that Rankin felt were beginning to dominate American life. Her militant feminism remained as strong as ever into the 1960s, prompting an attempt at establishing a self-sufficient cooperative for aging women at her homestead in Georgia.

Ever the loyal pacifist, Rankin became active again in the peace movement in the 1960s. Vehemently opposing the Vietnam War, she urged women to call for a stop to U.S. intervention in Vietnam. Even in her eighties, Rankin considered running for Congress in order to vote against appropriations. Instead she formed an all-women protest group known as the Jeannette Rankin Brigade, dedicated to nonviolent resistance of the war, and staged her last protest.

On January 15, 1968, at the age of eighty-seven, Jeannette Rankin led five thousand women from Union Station to the foot of the U.S. Capitol in a protest march against hostilities in Indochina. Marching with the brigade were Coretta Scott King and Dagmar Wilson, founder of the Women's Strike for Peace. Still fighting a year later, Rankin was part of the delegation that met with Speaker John McCormack and Senator Mike Mansfield.

During an interview with the press on her ninetieth birthday, the youthful Rankin talked about the penalties to women who chose the road of protest. "If they're independent, talkative, and say what they think, they can't get a job or a husband. Look at me—unmarried and unemployed most of my life!" When asked what she would do if she could live her life over again, Rankin answered, "This time I'd be nastier."

Ever true to her principles, Jeannette Rankin carried the torch for peace and women's rights until her death in 1973, two weeks before her ninety-third birthday.

GEORGIA O'KEEFFE

[1887–1986]

A revolutionary in the art world
and a pioneer in abstract art, O'Keeffe became one of the most
famous and productive artists of the twentieth century.
She found a home for her individuality
in the rugged landscape of the Southwest and led
women artists out of the classroom and into the world's
most prominent galleries and museums.

HE SLENDER, DARK-HAIRED woman stepped off the train into the blazing New Mexico sunshine. Squinting in the sun's glare, Georgia O'Keeffe looked off into the distance and gasped. The skies were so clear it seemed as if she could see forever, and the stark, lonely vistas stretching out before her were calling her home. Feeling its pull, O'Keeffe named the land "the faraway," and vowed to return. Years later, she would remember this day and say, "From then on, I was always on my way back."

For O'Keeffe, the passion for New Mexico remained as intense as it was on the day she arrived. For twenty-one years she would hurry back to spend the summer there, until 1950 when she was able to move permanently. The hills, desert, and mountains around Taos, New Mexico, inspired her life and work more than any other place she had ever lived. In turn, O'Keeffe portrayed its harsh scenery on canvas like no artist before her. Listening to her own inner voice, she painted as her feelings dictated, creating large, lucid paintings of unusual subjects, a single mission cross, a bleached cow's skull, or some other abandoned object she had picked up in the desert. O'Keeffe also never tired of painting the surrounding mountains and countless other Southwestern scenes during her long love affair with the American West.

GEORGIA O'KEEFFE *near "The Pink House," Taos, New Mexico, 1929. Courtesy Museum of New Mexico, 9763.*

Georgia Totto O'Keeffe, a remarkable woman who provided inspiration for other women artists, was born in 1887 into a large dairy-farming family in Sun Prairie, Wisconsin. When she was six, the family moved to Virginia, where Georgia's artistic talents were noticed and encouraged with several years of private art lessons at various schools. By the time she was in eighth grade, Georgia was certain she would be an artist someday. True to her word, after graduating from high school in 1905, she moved to Chicago to attend the Art Institute of Chicago.

Two years later O'Keeffe enrolled in the Art Student League in New York City, where she was awarded the League's still-life prize for an oil painting. A short time later, O'Keeffe became discouraged with the years spent studying classical art and felt the need for a new direction. When she learned of her family's financial problems, the twenty-one-year-old O'Keeffe left the League in search of a job.

She returned to Chicago and found work as a commercial artist at an advertising company, producing sketches for magazines and newspapers and designing lace and embroidery. Two years later, in 1914, a case of measles left her with eyes too weak to do her exacting, detailed job, and she was forced to resign and return to her family home in Virginia.

O'Keeffe did not feel inspired to create any original artwork until she enrolled in a summer art course at the University of Virginia. When her art professor, Alon Bement, introduced her to the revolutionary idea of expressing personal thoughts and feelings through harmonious arrangements of line, color, and light, O'Keeffe's creative fires were re-ignited, and she began producing in volume.

To support herself, O'Keeffe taught art in Amarillo, Texas, and returned in the summer to work as Bement's teaching assistant in Virginia. The bleak, flat land surrounding Amarillo stimulated O'Keeffe, and she began incorporating the exciting ideas she had learned from Bement into her classes and into her own work. In the fall of 1915, O'Keeffe was ready to discover her own personal style and began creating according to her feelings. She had to "strip away what I had been taught—and to accept as true my own thinking." The result was a series of abstract charcoal drawings that broke traditional rules of the time but later was considered among the most innovative of American art of the period. O'Keeffe mailed some of the drawings to a former classmate in New York, who then presented them to Alfred Stieglitz, an internationally known photographer and owner of the popular, avant-garde Gallery 291.

Stieglitz was considered a pioneer in the art of photography and one of the country's greatest photographers, and is also credited with introducing America to the works of Picasso, Matisse, and Cezanne at his controversial gallery. He responded to O'Keeffe's drawings with praise, considering them the "purest, finest, sincerest things that had entered 291 in a long while."

Eager to introduce a promising new American female artist to the art world, Stieglitz exhibited ten of O'Keeffe's drawings at his studio without bothering to consult the artist. When O'Keeffe heard about the showing, she confronted the gallery owner but agreed to leave them on display when Stieglitz praised her as the first American woman with the ability to express her feelings honestly in an abstract way on paper.

Although the show attracted attention to her controversial work, O'Keeffe still needed a means of support and returned to Texas in the fall of 1916 to teach art at West Texas State Normal College in Canyon, Texas. During her free time, O'Keeffe explored canyons, hiking down steep slopes to sandstone formations. She painted at least fifty watercolors during her time in northern Texas, a time she remembered as "so far away…there was quiet and an untouched feel to the country…" More than seven decades later, *Canyon Suite*, a collection of twenty-eight of O'Keeffe's paintings from her years in Texas, would be discovered wrapped in brown paper by the granddaughter of a college acquaintance to whom O'Keeffe had given the paintings before he left to serve in World War I.

A year after Stieglitz introduced O'Keeffe's work at his gallery, he arranged her first solo show, which featured mainly her watercolors from Texas. After the show, financial woes would force Stieglitz to close his gallery, but his interest and belief in O'Keeffe's work and talent would remain. He urged her to leave Texas and return to New York, offering financial support for a year so she could paint, an offer O'Keeffe accepted.

Although he was twenty-three years her senior, Stieglitz's role in O'Keeffe's life would change from mentor to lover to husband. When they chose to live together openly while Stieglitz was still married to his first wife, a scandal erupted. They married in 1924 after Stieglitz was divorced, when O'Keeffe was thirty-seven years old and Stieglitz was sixty-one. Married or not, O'Keeffe insisted on keeping her own name.

Stieglitz became obsessed with photographing the striking, slim, dark-haired O'Keeffe, and he shot more than three hundred portraits of her between 1918 and 1937. He was also her greatest supporter and promoter, and under his wise management, O'Keeffe became one of America's most important and successful artists by the mid-1920s, a time when women were expected only to teach art, not create it.

The couple spent many summer months at the Stieglitz family home at Lake

George in the Adirondack Mountains, a setting that aroused O'Keeffe's creative juices and inspired many paintings. Stieglitz took charge of her finished work and arranged shows, where he sold her paintings for handsome prices. The arrangement worked well, with the outgoing Stieglitz in the role of promoter and the reclusive O'Keeffe free to create her celebrated paintings, which she refused to autograph, but occasionally marked with an "OK."

During her long, prolific career, O'Keeffe moved from formal and abstract art with natural forms like flowers or shells to more rural subjects, such as barns and Mexican-Indian structures. Her best-known works, however, are her detailed, symbolic studies of flowers and desert, paintings often said to relate to female sexuality, an opinion O'Keeffe strongly disagreed with. Her paintings of oversized, single flowers, still her most popular, were a product of the long winters she spent in New York City. By using vivid colors and bold patterns, O'Keeffe created abstract designs so enormous and detailed they became unusual, sometimes even shocking. She explained, "Most people in the city rush around so, they have no time to look at a flower. I want them to see it whether they want to or not." Her first painting of a large flower, a calla lily, sold for $25,000 in 1925. The staggering amount earned O'Keeffe much attention, and convinced her that she could actually make a living as a serious artist.

Three years later, in 1928, O'Keeffe was restless again for new material to inspire her to meet the demands of an annual show. After listening to her friends' impressions of the Southwest, O'Keeffe decided to discover the West for herself. Because Stieglitz hated change and had no desire to leave New York, O'Keeffe traveled by train with a friend to spend the summer in Taos, New Mexico. It was a journey that changed her life and her work.

Each summer after her first visit, O'Keeffe returned to northern New Mexico to roam the desert, buttes, and mountains near Taos to search for fascinating objects. She discovered large wooden crosses alongside roads or adorning churches and learned that they had been erected by a secret religion that practiced flagellation and mock crucifixion. When she painted them later, she said, "Anyone who doesn't feel the crosses simply doesn't get that country." She collected abandoned, dry, white animal bones that were scattered across the desert and had them shipped back to New York, where she would later study them and capture them on canvas. She felt that the bones "cut sharply to the center of something that is keenly alive on the desert even tho' it is vast and empty and untouchable…and knows no kindness with all its beauty."

O'Keeffe explored the rugged mountains and deserts on her own in a Model A Ford that she had bought and had friends teach her how to drive. She removed

GEORGIA O'KEEFFE *residence, Ghost Ranch, near Abiquiu, New Mexico. Photo by John Candelario. Courtesy Museum of New Mexico, 165680.*

the back seat and unbolted the front seat, so she could stop where she liked, turning around and propping her canvas against the car's back wall, and paint the stunning vistas that surrounded her. When she visited the historical mission church at Ranchos de Taos, the subject of many artists before her, she painted only a portion of the mission wall silhouetted against a vivid, dark blue sky. When asked about the unusual fragmentary portrayal, she said, "it seemed to make my statement as well as or better than the whole could...I had to create an equivalent for what I felt about what I was looking at...not copy it."

She first visited the remote Ghost Ranch, 120 miles north of Albuquerque, in the summer of 1934. She claimed that "All the earth colors of the painter's palette are out there in the many miles of badlands," and knew that she would make her home there someday. She came to know the arts community that had developed in Taos, and she became friends with Ansel Adams, D. H. Lawrence, Spud Johnson, and other writers and artists who were drawn to the area.

In 1940 O'Keeffe did purchase a house at Ghost Ranch, and five years later she bought another in the tiny community of Abiquiu, sixteen miles away. She also claimed ownership of the Pedernal, a flat-topped mesa in the Jemez Mountain range, which stood within view of her home. She explained, "It's my private mountain. It belongs to me. God told me if I painted it enough, I could have it."

During the summer of 1946, Stieglitz suffered a cerebral thrombosis in New York. O'Keeffe immediately flew back to her husband's side, where she remained until he died several days later. After burying his ashes at the foot of a tall pine tree beside Lake George, she stayed to settle the affairs of Stieglitz's estate and oversee the distribution of his art collection. Then, in 1950, she returned to New Mexico to live the rest of her long, interesting life.

During the decade of the 1950s, the art world would be caught up in a period of transition, a time when O'Keeffe's work would be considered out of fashion. For the next twenty-five years, she would keep a low profile, painting and traveling extensively. It was during her travels to Mexico, South America, Europe, and Asia, that O'Keeffe became fascinated with the views from the window of an airplane. She began painting motifs of sky and clouds as seen from above, and in 1965, when she was seventy-eight years old, O'Keeffe created the largest work of her career, *Sky Above Clouds IV*, which measured twenty-four feet by eight feet.

In 1962, O'Keeffe was elected to the fifty-member American Academy of Arts and Letters, the nation's highest honor society for people in the arts, and by the 1970s, her work was beginning to receive renewed interest from a new generation of art fans. In demand again after a quarter of a century, O'Keeffe's work began appearing at prestigious galleries and museums across the country, setting new attendance records.

Unfortunately, during the decade of her rediscovery, O'Keeffe was in her eighties and her eyesight was failing. In 1971, the eighty-four-year-old artist was left with only peripheral sight, forcing her to stop painting the following year. She reconsidered her decision after a young potter named Juan Hamilton appeared at O'Keeffe's ranch house looking for work. After O'Keeffe hired him, Hamilton became her closest companion, helping her manage her business and inspiring her to create again, even with her dimming eyesight.

Renewed, O'Keeffe installed a large kiln at her ranch for firing pots and began dabbling in pottery. With Juan's help, she wrote her autobiography in 1976, and agreed to interviews and the filming of a documentary at her ranch. When asked about the subject of death, O'Keeffe said, "When I think of death, I only regret that I will not be able to see this beautiful country anymore…unless the Indians are right and my spirit will walk here after I'm gone."

As she entered her ninth decade, O'Keeffe became very frail and eventually moved to Santa Fe, where she died in 1986 at the age of ninety-eight. Per her instructions, O'Keeffe's body was cremated. Afterwards, Juan Hamilton walked her ashes to the top of Pedernal Mountain and scattered them to the winds over her beloved "faraway," the land where O'Keeffe's spirit is said to walk.

MARY PICKFORD

[1893–1979]

*No American movie actress symbolized
the age of innocence better than Mary Pickford.
Adored by her fans, the petite, baby-faced star
of the silent screen became America's first superstar
and the most famous woman in the world during her time.
What her many fans didn't know
was that behind the scenes, their sweet "Little Mary" was a
shrewd operator and a tyrant in the boardroom.*

ALTHOUGH SHE WAS A grown woman in her twenties, wide-eyed Mary Pickford bounced about the set in a ruffled dress and Mary Jane shoes, acting just like a child. Barely five feet tall, "the little girl with the golden curls" was doing exactly what her audience liked best, playing the part of a smiling, preadolescent girl, the role that brought the actress fame, fortune, and the nickname "America's Sweetheart." Unfortunately, the role that so captivated the public eventually became an albatross around Pickford's neck.

If ever an actress was a victim of typecasting, it was Mary Pickford. No matter what role she attempted to play during her prolific career, her fans preferred to see her frolicking about as a lovable young girl facing a hard, cruel world. They liked their "Little Mary" best in films like *Rebecca of Sunnybrook Farm*, in which the twenty-four-year-old Pickford played the lead, a plucky preteen who blended in perfectly with the cast of eleven and twelve year olds. By recognizing an opportunity when she saw one, Pickford capitalized on the childlike role her fans demanded and became the first millionaire actress in history.

MARY PICKFORD *became the first millionaire actress in history. Courtesy the Mary Pickford Library.*

Not wanting to tarnish her Little Mary image, Pickford wisely decided to downplay the fact that offscreen she was an ambitious, driven woman, who insisted on absolute control over every aspect of her career. She built an acting career that spanned twenty-four years and starred in more than two hundred films, many of which she produced herself. A tough-as-nails negotiator, Pickford was the first motion picture star to control her own work, dictate her own contracts, and co-found a company through which she produced, marketed, and distributed her own films. Using the shrewd business skills she learned from her mother, Pickford became one of the most powerful pioneers in the film industry during her time, a feat she accomplished while playing the part of a preadolescent girl.

The woman who became America's Sweetheart was born Gladys Louise Smith in 1892 in Toronto, Canada. The eldest of three children, Gladys was three years old when her father deserted the family. Without any means of support, her mother, Charlotte, converted a room in the family home into a rental. When a stage manager for a local theater company moved in, the life of the Smith family changed forever.

From their new tenant, the family was introduced to the world of the stage. They met actors and actresses and learned how they lived and how much they were paid for their performances. Recognizing the possibility that the theater could provide a way to escape the family's poverty, Charlotte encouraged her children to audition for children's roles.

All three Smith children would become stage performers, playing the parts of children. By the time she was eight years old, Gladys was appearing in her first melodrama. From the beginning, Gladys had felt at home on the stage. Excited by performing, she was neither afraid of the audience nor intimidated by other actors. In fact, little Gladys was so appealing on stage that she was often reprimanded for stealing scenes from other actors.

When Gladys was nine years old, her mother sold their Toronto home and, with her children, joined an American traveling theater company. After a tour through the Midwest and eastern sections of the United States, the family settled for awhile in New York, where Gladys and her siblings acted in stage productions.

In 1907, after two years spent performing in theaters in New York City, Gladys had become the major wage earner of the family. She was now ready to become a better actress and wanted to find a good director. Taking the bull by the horns, she arranged an audition with the most respected stage producer/director in the business, David Belasco. After their meeting, Belasco changed her name to Mary Pickford and agreed to transform fifteen-year-old Gladys from a performer into an actress.

MARY PICKFORD *starring in* REBECCA. *Courtesy the Mary Pickford Library.*

The new Mary Pickford had a small salary coming in, but money was still short for the Smith family. To supplement her income, she considered working in the "flickers," one-reel silent films shown in between stage productions.

After locating Biograph Studios, the leading film company in New York, Pickford signed a contract with D. W. Griffith, the pioneer film director credited with turning film into an art form.

Pickford didn't care if D. W. Griffith was considered the greatest filmmaker of the day. She was at Biograph simply to make a few dollars in a flicker or two. She was totally unaware that her ethereal presence, fragile body, romantic long curls, and large, expressive eyes were the very qualities that Griffith was searching for to capture on film.

Because she considered flickers much less important than stage acting, Pickford boldly announced to Griffith, "You must realize I'm an actress and an

Although PICKFORD *and* FAIRBANKS *were wary about public approval, they married in 1920 anyway. Courtesy the Mary Pickford Library.*

artist. I've had important parts on the real stage. I must have twenty-five a week guaranteed, and extra when I work extra." The spunky confidence impressed Griffith, who gave in to most of Pickford's demands and agreed to be her mentor and guide to the film world. Later Pickford would consider Griffith a great director and one of her greatest teachers.

After a year at Biograph Studios, Pickford was in demand at the nickelodeons. By the time she had completed two years under Griffith's direction, Pickford had appeared in seventy-nine silent films. With the film industry growing rapidly, many film companies headquartered in the East were relocating in southern

California, lured by the endless sunshine, rolling landscape, and cheap labor. When Biograph completed a film shoot in the Los Angeles area, the company also joined the migration to the West and opened a studio in 1910 in a small community called Hollywood.

When the popular Mary Pickford arrived in Hollywood, she was nineteen years old and known more for her silent films than for her stage performances. Rival film companies were making offers, and Pickford saw the chance to do some wheeling and dealing. After just a few months at Biograph's new facility in the West, she left for a higher salary at Independent Motion Picture Productions. During this time, Pickford married Owen Moore, a handsome Irish actor she had worked with at Biograph, a man of whom her mother disapproved. The marriage would eventually fail, unable to withstand the pressures of Moore's insecurity, Mary's growing fame, and her attachment to her mother.

Using her tough, ruthless business skills, Pickford spent the next two years switching from studio to studio, negotiating for more money with each move. By demanding equal footing with her leading film contemporary, Charlie Chaplin, Pickford was able to raise her earnings substantially. She would return to Biograph in 1912 and join Adolph Zukor's Famous Players Company the following year. All the moving around was worth the effort for Pickford, who watched her salary rise from $40 to an incredible $500 a week. A mere three years later, she was earning the staggering weekly sum of $10,000.

At Famous Players, which later became Paramount Pictures, Adolph Zukor starred Pickford in his new eight-reel feature movies. Two years later, after charming audiences in the role of a young, winsome girl, she had become the company's greatest asset and earned the nickname America's Sweetheart. Later, when she was asked why she played the part so well, Pickford said, "I was forced to live far beyond my years when just a child; now I have reversed the order and I intend to remain young indefinitely."

Bolstered by her popularity, Pickford began dictating the wording of her contracts and blazing the trail for the demands of other film stars. Her salary demands continued until they became too hefty for producers to earn a decent profit. When this happened, Pickford became her own producer, cofounding United Artists Corporation in 1919 with her old boss D. W. Griffith and fellow actors Charlie Chaplain and Douglas Fairbanks. Now in her mid-twenties, Pickford was an actress, director, executive producer, and studio owner with total control over her pictures. She was also in love.

Pickford had met Fairbanks, the dashing swashbuckler of the silent screen, a few years earlier during a nationwide celebrity tour promoting Liberty War Bonds. Although these two wildly popular stars were wary about the public's approval of their romance, they married anyway in 1920, after divorcing their former spouses.

As it turned out, they had nothing to worry about. As newlyweds, they were more popular than ever, mobbed wherever they went by cheering crowds anxious for a view of the world's most perfect couple. They reigned as the undisputed king and queen of Hollywood, throwing lavish parties attended by glittering celebrities and famous dignitaries at their elegant Beverly Hills mansion, Pickfair.

Pickford, now well into her twenties, was producing her own movies. Although she was eager for more challenging on-screen roles, she was constantly reminded that her audience wanted to see her in the same innocent roles, like the lead in *Pollyanna*, which she starred in and produced in 1920. She was very aware that the slightest misstep could ruin her box-office appeal. All she had to do was look back a few years to 1918, when she appeared in *Stella Maris*, a brilliant film that had been written for her, and in which she played two roles. To her disappointment, the public didn't support the film, preferring instead her portrayal of a smiling, preadolescent girl, a role Pickford would play into her thirties. She reasoned, "I didn't want what happened to Chaplin to happen to me. When he discarded the little tramp, the little tramp turned around and killed him."

But by the mid-1920s, the naughty Jazz Age "flappers" had arrived, boldly challenging women to drop their Victorian inhibitions. Aware that her sweet ingenue image was suddenly dated, Pickford attempted to grow up on camera by starring in adult dramas. She cut off her curls in 1929 and made her debut in the talking film *Coquette*, for which she would receive an Oscar. She played the testy Kate opposite her husband in Shakespeare's *The Taming of the Shrew* and starred in a contemporary comedy, *Kiki*.

All three films were box-office failures, proving to Pickford that she was imprisoned forever in the Little Mary image she had so expertly crafted. Even after she won an Academy Award for her work in *Coquette*, Pickford could not persuade her fans to accept her as a talking, adult actress. She decided to retire from acting in 1933, followed a year later by Fairbanks, both victims unable to make the transition to the new "talkies."

Pickford wasn't in front of the camera anymore, but she still had her share in United Artists and became involved in various projects. She gave radio broadcasts, started a cosmetic line, and helped to incorporate Beverly Hills. With her considerable influence, Pickford worked to secure insurance and retirement benefits for screen artists and to establish the Motion Picture Country Home and Hospital.

In 1936, after seven years of separation, Pickford ended her marriage to Fairbanks and married for the third and final time one year later. Her marriage to a former costar, Charles "Buddy" Rogers, lasted until her death, forty-three years later. In 1943, they adopted a six-year-old boy, Ronald, and a six-month-old girl, Roxanne. Along with her role as a mother, Pickford remained involved in film production for many years, holding onto her beloved United Artists until the early 1950s, when she and Chaplin finally sold their interests.

As she aged, Pickford became increasingly dependent on alcohol and lived a reclusive life behind the walls of Pickfair. She emerged in 1976 to attend the Academy Awards and receive a Lifetime Achievement Award for her service to the film industry. It was her last public appearance. She died three years later of a cerebral hemorrhage in Santa Monica, California, in 1979. She was eighty-seven years old.

Mary Pickford, a powerful pioneer in the mighty Hollywood movie industry, was also a revolutionary. Until she came along with her demands, film actors' names were kept hidden from the audience. Pickford removed the shackles of anonymity from herself and her fellow actors. Then she stunned the industry by cofounding, with three other film industry giants, a company that would give her the rights to produce, market, and distribute her own films. Yet, for all the power she would wield in Hollywood during the 1920s and '30s, Mary Pickford was never allowed to grow up on screen.

DOROTHEA LANGE

[1895–1965]

You put your camera around your neck
along with putting on your shoes,
and there it is,
an appendage of the body that shares your life with you.

—Dorothea Lange

HE STEADY FLIP-FLOP of the windshield wipers seemed to relax the driver as she gazed at the wet, shiny pavement that stretched ahead in a long, endless ribbon. Tired and anxious to finish the seven-hour drive home, she nearly missed the crude sign beside the road that said "Pea Pickers Camp." She slowed the car, made a U-turn, and drove back in the rain toward the sign.

Mud splattered from the tires as the car bounced along the dirt road leading to the camp, where rows of soggy tents and ragged shelters were slung across a muddy, barren field. In a dirty canvas lean-to at the far edge of the camp, a haggard-looking mother sat on a wooden box, nursing a baby and gazing worriedly into the distance. Two children came up behind her and buried their smudged faces in her bony shoulders.

The car slowed to a stop, and a woman climbed out with a bulky, box-shaped camera in her hands. She aimed her camera at the lean-to, focusing the lens on the gaunt mother and her children. Then, speaking softly so as not to wake the baby, she inched closer and clicked the camera's shutter.

Dorothea Lange, the woman with the camera, was following her instincts when she drove into the pea-pickers camp that rainy day in March 1936. She was a photographer, hired by the government to document the living and working conditions of the many farm workers who had fled devastating dust storms in

---

Portrait of DOROTHEA LANGE. *Courtesy the Dorothea Lange Collection, Oakland Museum of California. Lent by John Eaglefeather Dixon.*

the Midwest for California's agricultural fields. After a month spent photographing in the fields and migrant camps of Southern California's Imperial Valley area, Lange was on her way home with a suitcase full of images to send to Washington, D.C. She had only five exposures left in her camera.

Those last five photographs taken in the soggy field in Nipomo would become famous. The poignant images of the migrant mother and her children appeared in newspapers and magazines across the country, alerting the public to the desperate plight of the California migrant camps. Lange's photographs touched the hearts of the people and moved the government to send a shipment of twenty thousand pounds of food to the starving farm workers.

Through her camera's lens, Lange captured the unforgettable scenes of our nation's darkest hours. Her haunting photographs taken during the Great Depression revealed the hopelessness on the faces of jobless men standing in bread lines, and the pride and despair of sharecroppers and migrant workers. In her stark black-and-white images of the forced Japanese American relocation that followed the bombing of Pearl Harbor, she portrays the shame and sadness of one of the bleakest moments in our country's history.

Although the art world considered Dorothea Lange one of the greatest documentary photographers of the twentieth century, Lange never thought of herself as an artist. She didn't believe in asking her subjects to pose, nor did she include props for dramatic effect. She said, "Hands off! I do not molest what I photograph, I do not meddle and I do not arrange." Lange simply used her camera to candidly record the social upheaval of the time.

Born in the quiet town of Hoboken, New Jersey, in 1895, Dorothea Nutzhorn grew up on the Lower East Side of New York City. Her brother, Martin, was born six years later, a year before Dorothea was stricken with polio. The illness left Dorothea self-conscious about her permanent limp and profoundly sensitive to the plight of others. After her father abandoned the family, twelve-year-old Dorothea moved with her mother and brother to the home of her maternal grandmother. Her mother found work in the Lower East Side, and enrolled Dorothea in a school nearby. On the days when her mother worked late, Dorothea wandered the streets wearing an anonymous "cloak of invisibility" on her face, a technique that she would perfect during her career years.

Dorothea yearned to be a photographer before she ever held a camera in her hands, but her mother had other ideas and enrolled Dorothea in the New York Training School for Teachers. Although Dorothea attended the classes, she refused to let go of her dream. She found part-time work after class in the portrait studio of Arnold Genthe, a noted photographer and favorite of the rich and famous. Dorothea learned much about the techniques of portrait photography at

Genthe's studio, how to achieve proper lighting, how to manage the awkward cameras of the day, and how to cater to the whims of the wealthy. Hungry to learn more, Dorothea also found work at other studios and studied photography under Clarence White at Columbia University.

After deciding once and for all that she was not destined to be a teacher, Dorothea dropped out of school and bought her first camera, a bulky, box-like contraption with pleated bellows and two lenses. She learned to develop photographs in the darkroom she made in an unused chicken coop, and she soon had the skills necessary to launch her own business. But she wanted it to be far from Hoboken.

In 1918, when Dorothea was twenty-two, she talked a friend into taking a trip around the world with her. They made it as far as San Francisco, where a thief ran off with their money and left them with the need to find jobs. Happy to be as far away from the East Coast as possible, Dorothea was enthralled with the free-spirited city by the Bay. Impressed and inspired by the community's support of their local artists, she soon became part of a bohemian art crowd.

As she launched a new life in the West, Dorothea also decided to make a few other changes. Still smarting from her father's abandonment, she changed her last name to that of her mother, Lange, and to lessen her self-consciousness about her limp, Lange began wearing long skirts and a black beret. She also dreamed about opening her own portrait studio in the city.

Six months after she arrived in San Francisco, Dorothea met a wealthy investor who loaned her the money to open a studio. During the day, Lange photographed San Francisco's well-to-do women, while after hours she developed the images in her darkroom on the lower level. At night her studio filled with Lange's growing group of artsy, bohemian friends, including the forty-five-year-old Maynard Dixon, a handsome, rawboned cowboy artist who was twenty-one years her senior.

Lange was fascinated by the independent, adventurous Dixon and married him in 1920. They had two sons together before the marriage began to unravel due to Lange's overwhelming responsibilities of managing career and family and Dixon's lengthy solitary painting expeditions. In 1931, during one of their many attempts to improve the marriage, the family moved to Taos, New Mexico. The extended vacation allowed time for Dixon to paint and for Lange to document images of her children and Native Americans.

When the family returned to San Francisco several months later, the misery of the Great Depression years had set in. Moved by scenes she saw in the streets, Lange turned her camera from her portrait studio to the city streets. She developed a keen interest in social issues as she focused her lens on destitute men

DOROTHEA LANGE *and* MAYNARD DIXON *were married for fifteen years.*
Courtesy Arnold Genthe Collection, Library of Congress.

waiting at soup kitchens and standing in bread lines and on groups of down-and-outers huddled on street corners. She toted her camera down to the waterfront, where she blended into the crowd and photographed angry dockworkers on strike.

The collection of photographs Lange made during the Depression years attracted the attention of critics across the country and the admiration of Paul Schuster Taylor, a labor economist and professor at the University of California at Berkeley. Lange agreed to work with Taylor on an assignment for the California State Emergency Relief Administration, to document the living conditions of the many migrant workers who had fled the drought and unemployment in the Midwest for better conditions in California. Strapping their belongings onto their cars, the migrant families headed to the Imperial Valley in Southern California with dreams of finding available farmland. What they found, however, were more desperate migrants vying for jobs as crop pickers on land belonging to others.

As she worked, Lange gently immersed herself into the lives of the migrants, asking questions and moving quietly through fields where entire families toiled together in the blazing sun. In time, the workers relaxed and felt comfortable enough with Lange and her camera to resume their picking.

Lange recorded the deplorable conditions, the dirty irrigation water used for cooking and washing, the ramshackle camps set up on the banks of irrigation ditches, and the crowded relief offices. The combination of Taylor's convincing essays and Lange's haunting photographs brought help to the migrant workers through the establishment of state-built migrant camps. Their work also resulted in the book *An American Exodus: A Record of Human Erosion*, which was published in 1939.

After living separately for a number of years, Lange and Dixon ended their fifteen-year marriage in 1933. A few months later, Lange and Taylor were married. In 1935 Lange received an invitation to join a select group of photographers working for the Farm Security Administration (FSA) in Washington, D.C. Unlike the others in the group, Lange did not relocate to Washington, but stayed in her Berkeley home, which she used as her base of operations. The FSA photographers were hired to investigate America's westward development and to document living conditions in the poor rural areas. This four-year assignment provided the stage for Lange's landmark work, which she accomplished with an unwavering eye, capturing on film the harsh poverty, the hopelessness and despair, and the pride and dignity of the poverty-stricken farm workers and their families.

One such image, *Migrant Mother*, would become Lange's most recognized, illustrating the depth of emotion that can be conveyed through a photograph. In the portrait, a gaunt migrant woman, her face prematurely marked by wrinkles, holds a sleeping baby on her lap and gazes worriedly into the distance. Two older children lean against her shoulders, hiding their faces from the camera. Later Lange would say:

> *I saw and approached the hungry and desperate mother, as if drawn by a magnet. I do not remember how I explained my presence or my camera to her, but I do remember she asked me no questions. I made five exposures, working closer and closer from the same direction. I did not ask her name or her history. She told me her age, that she was thirty-two. She said they had been living on frozen vegetables from the surrounding fields, and birds that the children killed. She had just sold the tires from her car to buy food. There she sat in that lean-to tent with her children huddled around her, and seemed to know that my pictures might help her, and so she helped me. There was a sort of equality about it.*

Migrant Mother exposed the plight of the migrant farm workers and was reproduced numerous times all over the world. The powerful image would also symbolized forever the despair of the Great Depression years in the United States and inspired the making of the film, *Grapes of Wrath*.

By the 1940s, photographers were using the new lightweight 35mm cameras that allowed them to take thirty-six photographs before reloading. Lange, however, continued to work with her cumbersome Graflex, which needed to be reloaded after each shot. Uninterested in speed or aggression, she believed that her subjects should be a part of the photographic process, and that a photographer stole the spirit of the subject by shooting quickly and aggressively.

When her work with the FSA ended, a new door would open in Lange's life as a photographer with the coming of World War II. In 1942, three months after the attack on Pearl Harbor, she would experience the human impact of a whole new series of social and political changes in the American West. When President Franklin Roosevelt issued Executive Order 9066 ordering the forced relocation of Japanese Americans into armed camps in the Western interior, Lange was among the group of photographers hired by the Office of War Information and the War Relocation Authority to document the relocation.

Lange's earlier work with displaced farm families and migrant workers during the Great Depression had not prepared her for the disturbing racial and civil rights issues raised by the Japanese relocation program. As she photographed the uprooting and evacuation of San Francisco's Japanese neighborhoods, the anti-Japanese public policies, the processing centers and camps, Lange quickly found herself at odds with her employer and the United States government.

To illustrate life in the actual relocation camps, Lange created images that often blended signs of human courage and dignity with physical evidence of the indignities of the forced incarceration. With her compassionate heart and professional eye, Lange used a realistic approach while photographing in the internment camps. Her sympathetic images, which addressed the question of civil rights of the Japanese American citizens, were not appreciated back in Washington, resulting in the impounding of many of her photographs.

The true impact of her war relocation work was not felt until 1972, when the Whitney Museum incorporated twenty-seven of her photographs into an exhibit about the Japanese relocation. A *New York Times* critic called Lange's photographs "documents of such a high order that they convey the feelings of the victims as well as the facts of the crime."

Lange's home in Berkeley was located a few miles away from the Richmond shipyards, which had become the largest shipbuilding industry in the world during the war. More than 240,000 people, many former migrant farm workers, labored around the clock to keep the production of ships moving. In 1944 Lange joined her friend and noted photographer, Ansel Adams, on a photographic assignment at the Richmond shipyards for *Fortune Magazine*.

After the war, Lange's career was frequently interrupted by illness, but she remained dedicated to and driven by her work. She photographed the United Nations conference in San Francisco for the State Department, and shot photos in Ireland and Asia for *Life* magazine. Lange was the first woman to receive a Guggenheim Foundation grant, which allowed her to study and photograph the Mormon, Shaker, and Amish communities in the West and Midwest. In the 1950s and 1960s, Lange traveled around the world with her husband before settling down to photograph her family and people and places around her Berkeley home.

Dorothea Lange died from cancer in 1965 at age seventy. Within months of her death, the Museum of Modern Art in New York opened a major retrospective exhibition of her work. It was the museum's first exhibit to feature a woman photographer, signifying the enduring nature of Lange's images. After her death Lange's husband, Paul Taylor, donated an archive of some twenty-five thousand negatives and six thousand vintage prints to the Oakland Museum of California.

Lange dedicated much of her life to documenting change and its human cost through dramatic black-and-white photographs. To view Lange's work is to understand what it was like to be poor and desperate, yet full of dignity, and how it felt to be forced from your home and sent to prison camps because of your race. The themes Dorothea Lange photographed more than a half-century ago continue to touch our hearts today, showing us how the issues of her day, like those of ours, can impact the human spirit.

JACQUELINE COCHRAN

[ca. 1906–1980]

*Each flying record that Jackie Cochran shattered
drove her to break more and more,
until she was soaring higher and faster than any other woman
on the aviation frontier.*

ITH ONLY A FEW MINUTES' worth of fuel left in her tanks, Jackie Cochran zoomed her shiny silver P-35 across the finish line to win the prestigious 1938 transcontinental Bendix Air Race. Cochran had just completed the 2,042-mile race from Los Angeles to Cleveland, the first woman ever to win the race and the first pilot to finish the course without a stop. During the same year, this daring young woman entered more races and won more awards, setting the stage for her extraordinary career as a champion aviator.

The life of Jacqueline Cochran has all the makings of a best-selling novel, with a rags-to-riches rise from poor orphan girl to decorated airplane pilot, daring flying adventures, travel, and romance. But the remarkable story of this determined self-made woman who chose her own name, designed her own life, and opened the skies to women aviators is not a work of fiction. It is a true story.

The greatest woman pilot who ever lived was born sometime between 1906 and 1910 in northwestern Florida. Orphaned before she was four years old, blonde, brown-eyed little Jackie had no memory of her parents and never knew why she had been abandoned. She was sent to live with a poor migrant family in one of the area's sawmill towns in a shack with no plumbing, heat, or electricity, built on stilts near a swamp. During her bleak childhood, Jackie dreamed of a better life and somehow developed the self-confidence needed to force her dreams to come true.

JACQUELINE COCHRAN *was known as the greatest woman pilot who ever lived. Courtesy the photo collection of the International Women's Air and Space Museum.*

When she was eight years old, her foster family migrated to Georgia to work in the cotton mills. Jackie dropped out of second grade, found a job at the mill, and became self-supporting, like the other members of the family. Although she never returned to school, Jackie taught herself to read and write by figuring out words on the boxcars of passing trains.

When the cotton season ended and the family prepared to move back to the sawmills of Florida, ten-year-old Jackie had other ideas. She found a job cleaning beauty shops and remained in Georgia. Three years later, Jackie had learned the beauty trade and was cutting hair professionally. Although she enjoyed her job, Jackie was persuaded by one of her customers "to do more with her life" by becoming a nurse. After three years of nurse's training, Jackie was still uncomfortable at the sight of blood and decided she was of more help to people in a beauty shop than a hospital.

Happy to be back in the beauty industry, Jackie attended training programs, where she learned how to make wigs and apply the newest rage, a permanent wave. She sharpened her skills in beauty shops in Montgomery, Alabama, and Pensacola, Florida, and soon Jackie became restless to move on to something bigger. When she found the name "Cochran" listed in a phone book, she claimed it as her own and decided to create an exciting life to go with it. Off she went to New York, the biggest city she knew of, where she landed a job in an elegant beauty salon at Saks Fifth Avenue department store.

The salon attracted many of the city's well heeled, who befriended Jackie Cochran and invited her to their social affairs. At one such event she met Floyd Odlum, a Wall Street millionaire and Cochran's future husband. When she revealed her dream of starting her own cosmetic company someday, Odlum replied that she would need wings to beat her competition. Cochran followed the advice and signed up for flying lessons at Roosevelt Field Flying School in Long Island.

Cochran said about the experience: "When I paid for my first lesson, a beauty operator ceased to exist and an aviator was born." She thoroughly enjoyed the flying lessons and learned quickly. During her third lesson, her instructor turned the airplane, a Fleet trainer with a sixty-horsepower engine, over to Cochran to fly alone. During her first solo flight, the engine stopped, forcing Cochran to land, a feat she performed well enough to impress her instructor, who called her "a born flyer." Three weeks later, Jackie Cochran had a pilot's license in her hand and flying in her blood.

New York's winter weather conditions often made flying impossible, and Cochran was enthusiastic to improve her skills in the cockpit. After reading an article in an aviation magazine that promoted the long flying season and endless blue skies in San Diego, California, Cochran packed up her belongings and moved to the West Coast.

Cochran arrived in the West at a time when the aviation industry was young and in the process of establishing an empire in Southern California. Within a few decades, the country's greatest concentration of aircraft factories and airplane manufacturing companies like Lockheed, Douglas, and Boeing would be centered in huge facilities located near San Diego and Los Angeles. It was the perfect place for an ambitious aviator.

After she was settled in San Diego, Cochran met several Navy pilots who agreed to teach her the Navy's method of flying if she would furnish the plane. Cochran bought a used TravelAir and spent the rest of the year mastering the technical aspects of aviation and navigation the Navy way. She practiced takeoffs and landings all over the deserted beaches and deserts of southern California. During one of her practice sessions, Cochran flew over the Coachella Valley of southeastern California. The sight of the vast desert landscape impressed her so much, she bought a twenty-acre parcel near the town of Indio. Later Cochran said that the day she spotted the Coachella Valley was the day she found her home.

After Cochran earned her advanced instrument and commercial pilot's licenses, she put her energies into realizing her dream of creating a cosmetic company. In 1935 the Jacqueline Cochran Cosmetic Company was launched with a beauty salon in Chicago, a chemist and a laboratory in New Jersey, and Cochran flying between the two locations and delivering her products to buyers all over the country. The company's best-selling product, moisturizing cream called Flowing Velvet, was created by Cochran to relieve the skin problems she encountered when flying long distances at high altitudes.

With her cosmetic company established, Cochran was eager to return to the cockpit and test her flying skills. She attempted to enter the 1934 Bendix cross-country air race from Los Angeles, California, to Cleveland, Ohio, the outstanding long-distance air race of the world, which offered $30,000 in prize money. When Cochran learned that the race was only open to male pilots, she challenged the policy but was unable to convince race officials to open the contest to women aviators. The persistent Cochran then took her argument to Vincent Bendix, the race's namesake and owner of the Bendix airplane manufacturing company, who was finally persuaded to open the race to female aviators.

Cochran suffered disappointment again when she tried to put her new commercial pilot's license to use and found that women were not allowed to pilot commercial airplanes. She decided to find other ways to make a living in an airplane and joined a flying circus, which provided her with an income and allowed her to practice for more flying competitions. Aviation races were held

JACQUELINE COCHRAN *in front of a Staggerwing Beech 1937. Courtesy the photo collection of the International Women's Air and Space Museum.*

around the country on a regular basis, with substantial prize money awarded to daring test pilots willing to fly experimental planes faster and farther than the present record holder. Although danger was involved, a winning pilot could count on instant fame and a hefty purse. Cochran knew she was a risk-taker and would be a good competitor, but she soon learned that some of the best races with the highest purses did not allow women to participate.

The first attempts at air racing were frustrating for Cochran, who was grounded with mechanical problems in a 1934 race from London, England, to Melbourne, Australia. A similar situation occurred a year later when Cochran entered the 1935 Bendix Race. After leaving Los Angeles bound for Cleveland, Cochran ran into engine problems over the Grand Canyon, forcing her to turn back.

By the mid 1930s, Cochran not only had flying in her blood, she had a bad case of racing fever and was determined to conquer the skies. She soon began setting speed and altitude records in the women's west-to-east transcontinental flights. By the end of the decade, Cochran was honored as the outstanding woman flier in the world.

In 1936 Jackie Cochran married Floyd Odlum, fourteen years her senior, in a secret ceremony in Kingman, Arizona. Cochran insisted on keeping her own name, claiming its recognition in aviation circles and at her successful cosmetics company. Odlum also owned property in Coachella Valley, so the couple merged both parcels, forming the eight-hundred-acre Cochran-Odlum Ranch, where they built a spacious estate with a nine-hole golf course and Olympic-size swimming pool.

During the forty years Cochran and Odlum lived in the Coachella Valley, they welcomed countless celebrities and dignitaries into their home. Among their houseguests was the famous aviatrix Amelia Earhart, who stayed at the ranch shortly before her fateful attempt to fly around the world. Other guests who spent time at the Cochran-Odlum Ranch were Howard Hughes, President Dwight Eisenhower, President Lyndon Johnson, General Chuck Yeager, and Walter Cronkite.

Cochran's competitive nature and fearless spirit of adventure made her an excellent test pilot. In 1937, she broke a record by taking a small, fabric-covered biplane to an altitude of thirty-three thousand feet, even though she suffered from frostbite and freezing conditions. When she came in third in the 1937 Bendix cross-country race, Cochran was hailed as the fastest female flyer and was sought out by a leading airplane manufacturer to fly a civilian version of the company's P-35 fighter plane. Cochran accepted the offer and the following year flew the A-16 to victory, winning the Bendix race in 1938, the only female in the race.

Cochran was also the only pilot to make race officials wait while she combed her hair and applied fresh makeup from her cosmetic bag. An hour later she was winging her way to New York for the women's transcontinental race, where she set cross-country records. The flying speed queen would continue to set records in races and contests all over the world, while the winds of World War II swirled on the horizon.

At the onset of the war Cochran began testing new aviation equipment that was being developed for war use. She tried hard to promote the use of women pilots in the Army Air Corps, but politicians and military officers ignored her. They argued that women were not physically strong enough to pilot heavy aircraft. Cochran would prove them wrong in 1941 by flying a bomber across the Atlantic Ocean from Canada to England.

It was the British, desperately short of World War II pilots, who proved that women could fly military aircraft by using female aviators to ferry war planes around the British Isles. Inspired by the program, Cochran went to London to meet with program officials and study the operation. When she returned to the U.S., she met with President Franklin Roosevelt and Eleanor Roosevelt to discuss the possibility of creating a similar program for American women pilots. Unable to gather support in the United States, Cochran realized that women were not wanted in the U.S. war effort, so she gathered up twenty-five of the best female aviators she knew and went to England, where they were needed to ferry planes for the British Air Transport Auxiliary (ATA). Cochran was out to prove that American women pilots were just as capable as their English counterparts.

As she had hoped, the success of the British ATA program did convince the U.S. Army Air Force to consider a similar program, and Cochran was asked to return to the United States and create it. In July 1943 Cochran was named Director of Flight Training for the Women's Air Force Service Pilots (WASP) at a facility located near Houston, Texas. Stories about Cochran's success in the war effort appeared in newspapers across the country, prompting twenty-five thousand women to apply for WASP training.

Cochran's female pilots trained B-17 turret gunners, worked as test pilots at repair depots, trained staff pilots at navigator schools, and piloted war planes and bombers across the Atlantic Ocean to Europe. By the war's end in 1944, more than one thousand WASP auxiliary pilots had delivered more than 12,600 planes, flown more than seventy-five different types of aircraft and logged over sixty million miles in the air. They also wore uniforms designed by Bergdorf-Goodman's and paid for by Cochran.

At the end of the war, Cochran became the first civilian woman to be commissioned a lieutenant colonel in the Air Force Reserves. She also fought hard to have the WASP admitted to the military on a permanent basis. But Congress voted against it and disbanded the WASP after the war. For her contribution, Cochran was awarded the Distinguished Service Medal in 1945. She proudly announced, "What the WASP have done is without precedent in the history of the world."

Although she was bitterly disappointed about the demise of the WASP, Cochran's flying career was far from over. In 1946 she entered the Bendix Race again, winning second place. A few years later, Cochran claimed a new speed record for propeller-driven aircraft and a new title, Aviatrix of the Decade.

When jet-powered aircraft arrived in the early 1950s, Cochran was eager to make the transition from the "props." She entered the jet age with the help of her friend, test pilot Chuck Yeager, who trained Cochran in the fastest airplanes in the world. Takeoffs and landings were perfected at the official Edwards Air Force Base, located north of her ranch in the Coachella Valley. In 1953, she became the first woman to break the sound barrier, traveling at 625.5 miles per hour in a jet powered F-86, a record that earned Cochran entry into the previously male dominated "supersonic club." The following year, Cochran published her autobiography, *The Stars at Noon*.

In the 1960s Cochran would set nine international jet records and hold more speed records than any other pilot in the world, male or female. She would become the first woman to fly a jet across the Atlantic, and in 1964 she would fly at 1,429 miles per hour, twice the speed of sound. Cochran also set more records, flying F-104G Starfighter jets in excess of 1,200 miles per hour.

Cochran was elected president of the Fédération Aéronautique Internationale and the National Aeronautic Association, and became a consultant to NASA. By the end of the decade, she was known as "the fastest woman in the world" with more than two hundred awards and trophies. In 1971 she became the first woman enshrined in the Aviation Hall of Fame.

Jackie Cochran was finally grounded in the early seventies when doctors announced that she needed a pacemaker and must say good-bye to her aviation career. No longer able to soar through the heavens, Cochran lived the remainder of her life outside the cockpit on her ranch in southern California. After her husband's death in 1976, Cochran's spirit and health began to wane. She died in 1980 and was buried while jets soared overhead.

Jacqueline Cochran was a visionary who believed a woman's place was in the sky or wherever she wanted it to be. Confident that women were as capable in a cockpit as men were, Cochran devoted much of her life to the advancement of women's roles in the aerospace industry and led the way by setting countless flying records throughout the world. But it was during the long flying seasons in the American West that Jackie Cochran soared through clear, blue skies, flying higher and faster than any other woman, becoming the greatest woman pilot who ever lived.

MILDRED BABE DIDRIKSON ZAHARIAS

[1914–1956]

Considered the greatest female athlete of all time,
Babe Didrikson challenged social customs
during a time when women were expected to comply
to a particular stereotype.
By setting records in an arena previously known only to men,
the extraordinary athlete from Texas
opened the world of competitive sports to women.

CROWD OF THOUSANDS thundered its applause for the lanky young woman from Texas, who had suddenly become the talk of the sports world. Twenty-one-year-old Babe Didrikson had just been awarded three medals, two gold and one silver, at the 1932 Olympic Games in Los Angeles. She had set a world record in javelin throwing, won the 80-meter hurdle, and placed second in the high jump, providing a country mired in the depths of the Great Depression with some much-needed inspiration. The spunky medalist and champion of many sports also gave the adoring public something to chuckle about when she answered a sportswriter who had asked if there was anything she didn't play. Didrikson said, "Yeah, dolls."

While the other girls in her neighborhood played with their dolls, Babe was outdoors with the boys, running, jumping, shooting basketballs, playing tennis, polo, soccer, lacrosse, or marbles. A scrappy tomboy during her youth, she earned the nickname "Babe" (after baseball hero Babe Ruth) for the many home runs she hit in sandlot baseball games. Muscular and well-coordinated, Didrikson

MILDRED "BABE" DIDRIKSON ZAHARIAS *knew even before her teens that she wanted to be "the greatest athlete that ever lived." Courtesy Library of Congress.*

excelled in every sport she tried, and she tried them all. She could dive, shoot, pitch, ride, bat, kick, fence, pass, bowl, skate, and even dance and play the harmonica. Didrikson wrote years later in her autobiography that she had no doubt about what she would do later in her life. "Before I was even into my teens, I knew what I wanted to be when I grew up…the greatest athlete that ever lived."

Mildred Ella Didrikson was born in Port Arthur, Texas, in 1914 to Norwegian parents who had immigrated to the United States in 1908. Her father, a sailor and carpenter, believed in the benefits of exercise and encouraged his family to use the wooden gym set he had built. In 1915, after a hurricane devastated Port Arthur and flooded their home, the family moved to the nearby oil town of Beaumont.

While growing up in the city's rugged south end, Didrikson began to show a preference and proficiency for sports and avoided traditional feminine pursuits. Aggressive and feisty, she had a slender, well-coordinated body and chose to wear masculine clothing and a short hair cut. Academics did not interest Didrikson, a poor student who worked only to stay eligible for athletic competition. Her focus and energy were aimed on the athletic field, where she had no equal. She participated on all the women's teams, baseball, basketball, golf, swimming, tennis, and volleyball, and would have joined the football team if the school would have allowed it. Determined to excel in every sport she tried, Didrikson was never satisfied unless she or her team came in first. Her best sport, basketball, was the most popular women's sport of the era, and during the years Babe played, her high school team never lost a game.

In 1930, during her last year in high school, the Employers Casualty Insurance Company in Dallas offered Babe a job and a place on the company's Golden Cyclone basketball team. With the promise of a very generous salary of $900 a year, Babe dropped out of high school before finishing and moved to Dallas to work as a stenographer at the insurance company. When she wasn't working, Babe underwent an intense training program and competed in athletics. For the next three years, Didrikson became the All-American women's basketball player. She led the Golden Cyclones to the national championship in 1931, often scoring thirty or more points at a time when a team score of twenty for a game was considered respectable.

Babe also participated in softball events, excelling as a pitcher and batting over .400 in the Dallas city league. When she attended a track meet for the first time, she became interested in javelin throwing and the hurdles, which reminded her of all the hedge jumping she did during her childhood. She joined the Golden Cyclone track team in 1930, and with Babe's innate athletic ability and

BABE *often scored thirty or more points at a time when a team score of twenty for a game was considered respectable. Courtesy Library of Congress.*

the expert coaching provided by the company, she became the premier women's track-and-field performer in the nation.

Babe held American, Olympic, or world records in five different track-and-field events, and stunned the athletic world in July 1932 at the national amateur track meet for women. After entering as the only member from the Golden Cyclone team, she scored thirty points and won the national women's team championship. She went on to win six gold medals and broke four world records in a single afternoon, the most incredible performance by any male or female in the annals of track-and-field history. An immediate sports star, Didrikson was featured on every sports page in the nation and became a member of the 1932 United States Olympic team.

After her stunning success at the 1932 Olympics, the leading sportswriter of the day, Grantland Rice, would describe her as "the most flawless section of muscle harmony, of complete mental and physical coordination the world of sport has ever known." When she returned to Texas, Didrikson was given a hero's welcome, with a parade through the confetti-filled streets of Dallas in a limousine piled high with red roses. By year's end, Babe Didrikson had been voted Woman Athlete of the Year by the Associated Press, an award she would win five more times—in 1945, 1946, 1947, 1950, and 1954.

As a woman competing in sports, Babe raised many eyebrows. By refusing to conform in her dress, speech, and manner to the ladylike image expected of female athletes, she suffered for her behavior with insidious rumors and innuendoes concerning her sex and femininity. Her disinterest in women's current fashion led to a sports-page article remarking on her "almost complete absence of feminine frills."

The attacks rolled right off Babe's back as she concentrated on using her remarkable athletic ability to earn the fame and fortune she deserved. Babe had no use for social niceties or phoniness, and her brash and outspoken behavior often provided good copy for a grateful press.

Babe was the darling of the media and the public, but she was a thorn in the side of many of her teammates, who considered her a pushy, ruthless, overbearing braggart. It was a time when athletes were expected to be modest and self-effacing, but Babe knew she was the best and often said so. Competitors accused her of not being a team player, and of wanting "to beat everybody in sight," but Babe interpreted the criticism as jealousy and resentment over her success.

When a controversy erupted with the Amateur Athletic Union over her amateur status, Babe was forced to become a professional. To earn a living, she engaged in promotional advertising and made personal appearances. She performed athletic feats and played her harmonica on stage, played exhibition basketball games and billiard matches, and organized a professional basketball team, "Babe Didrikson's All-Americans." The team of four men and three women toured the back roads of America, stopping in rural areas to challenge the local teams, and winning two out of every three games they played.

In Florida, Babe appeared in major league exhibition baseball games during spring training of 1934, and played for the famous House of David barnstorming baseball team. As a professional athlete, the cocky, confident Didrikson was at the peak of her career, earning several thousand dollars each month, a hefty sum for anyone in the Depression years.

After their first meeting, DIDRIKSON *and* ZAHARIAS *became inseparable and married several months later. Courtesy Library of Congress.*

Although Babe was recognized as an extraordinary athlete, she still faced criticism by those in the press and public who disapproved of women's involvement in professional sports. When Didrikson lost a billiards match to a female billiard champion, a sportswriter in New York used the opportunity to attack all female athletes by writing, "It would be much better if Didrikson and her ilk stayed at home, got themselves prettied up and waited for the phone to ring."

After two years on the professional circuit, Didrikson tired of providing the entertainment at exhibition games and stage appearances. Anxious to be taken seriously again as a competitive athlete, she pulled herself off the circuit and developed an interest in golf. In 1933, she moved to California to learn all she could about the game and began an obsessive training program. She spent eight to ten hours a day on the driving range, her hands blistered and bleeding from hitting more than a thousand balls a day.

When money finally ran out, twenty-three-year-old Didrikson returned to Texas and signed up to play in her first golf tournament. She shot a 77 and won a qualifying medal, and was dubbed "Wonder Girl" in the Texas newspapers. But when she won the Texas Women's Amateur Championship the following year, the United States Golf Association (USGA) declared Didrikson a professional and banned her from amateur golf. With few golf tournaments open to professionals, the disappointed Didrikson was forced to play exhibition golf matches and tour with professional golfers.

American sportswomen in the mid-1930s were expected to be soft and submissive, unlike the outspoken, muscular, and strong Didrikson. The fact that she could drive a ball three hundred yards, farther than most men, left many people feeling uncomfortable. But as she matured, Babe mellowed and began bending to society's dictates by growing her hair longer and wearing dresses and makeup. But even though her outward appearance appeared more feminine, Babe never gave up her competitive spirit and fierce determination to win.

In 1938, Babe entered the traditional male-dominated Los Angeles Open and caused quite a stir, although nowhere was it written that women could not compete. After she qualified, Babe was assigned playing partners, one a six-foot tall, three-hundred-pound professional wrestler named George Zaharias. After that first meeting, the twenty-eight-year-old Didrikson and Zaharias, thirty-seven, became inseparable and married several months later. The marriage finally silenced the attacks on Babe's femininity, including rumors that she was actually a male.

Both champions continued to work, but Zaharias, already a millionaire, retired from the ring a year after the marriage to manage his wife's promising career. Under her husband's management and direction, Babe won the 1940 Texas and Western Open golf tournaments. Afterwards, they both agreed that the only way to reach the top in women's golf was to play as an amateur.

To get her amateur standing back, Babe had to follow two rules. She needed letters of endorsement, and she had to wait for three years without accepting any payment for play or commercial endorsements. The wait was hard for the restless, competitive Babe, who filled the time bowling and playing tennis. With a wealthy husband supporting her, Babe easily met the USGA conditions and had her amateur standing restored in 1943.

After World War II, Babe Zaharias became one of the most successful and popular women golfers in history. She played flawless golf on the amateur tour and was presented with the Woman Athlete of the Year award for the second time. The following year, she established a record of victories in a string of consecutive tournaments that has never been equaled by man or woman. She would continue to dominate tournaments, including the British Women's Amateur, the first American to ever win the prestigious event. When asked by a British journalist how she was able to drive her ball such great distances, Babe wisecracked, "I just loosen my girdle and let the ball have it."

After her win at the British Open, the offers rolled in, many too tempting for Babe to refuse. So in 1947 she returned to the professional circuit again and earned an estimated $100,000 a year through promotions and exhibitions. At thirty-six, she was back on top with her name firmly carved into the sports world. But prize money on the professional golf tour only amounted to $3,400, despite a successful season.

In order to raise the tournaments' prize money and to popularize women's golf, Babe helped organize the Ladies Professional Golfer's Association (LPGA) in 1948. During the next several years, as the LPGA grew, Babe became the leading money winner on the women's professional circuit. She also involved herself in other ventures, exhibition games, and promotional events and worked as a teaching pro at two country clubs. In 1952, she even played the part of a golf champion in the movie *Pat and Mike*, starring Katharine Hepburn and Spencer Tracy.

Babe would require surgery for a hernia in her left thigh in the early 1950s and soon returned to the circuit. She continued to win tournaments but began to experience feelings of exhaustion. In the spring of 1953, after winning a tournament in her hometown, Babe went to her doctor for a checkup. The diagnosis was cancer, with radical surgery recommended. During the operation to remove the tumor, doctors discovered that the cancer had spread into the lymph nodes, a finding the doctors did not share with Babe.

Letters and telegrams poured in from fans around the world with wishes for Zaharias's quick recovery. Many feared that her career was over when doctors said the illness would leave her unable to play championship golf again. But the gritty Zaharias proved them wrong by appearing back on the circuit fourteen weeks after the surgery. A year later, with the sports world watching, Zaharias won a string of five tournaments, including the Women's Open. For the sixth time she was voted Outstanding Woman Athlete of the Year and was invited to the White House to help President Dwight Eisenhower launch a Cancer Crusade fund drive.

Two years after her diagnosis, in 1955, the cancer returned, this time with excruciating pain. But despite the pain, Babe still played an occasional round of golf and completed her autobiography before her death in Galveston in 1956.

Athletes, celebrities, and fans around the world mourned the passing of this courageous woman from Texas, a remarkable athlete and a tough competitor. Even in her final illness, Babe Didrikson Zaharias displayed the kind of strength and determination that marked her phenomenal career and opened competitive professional sports to women.

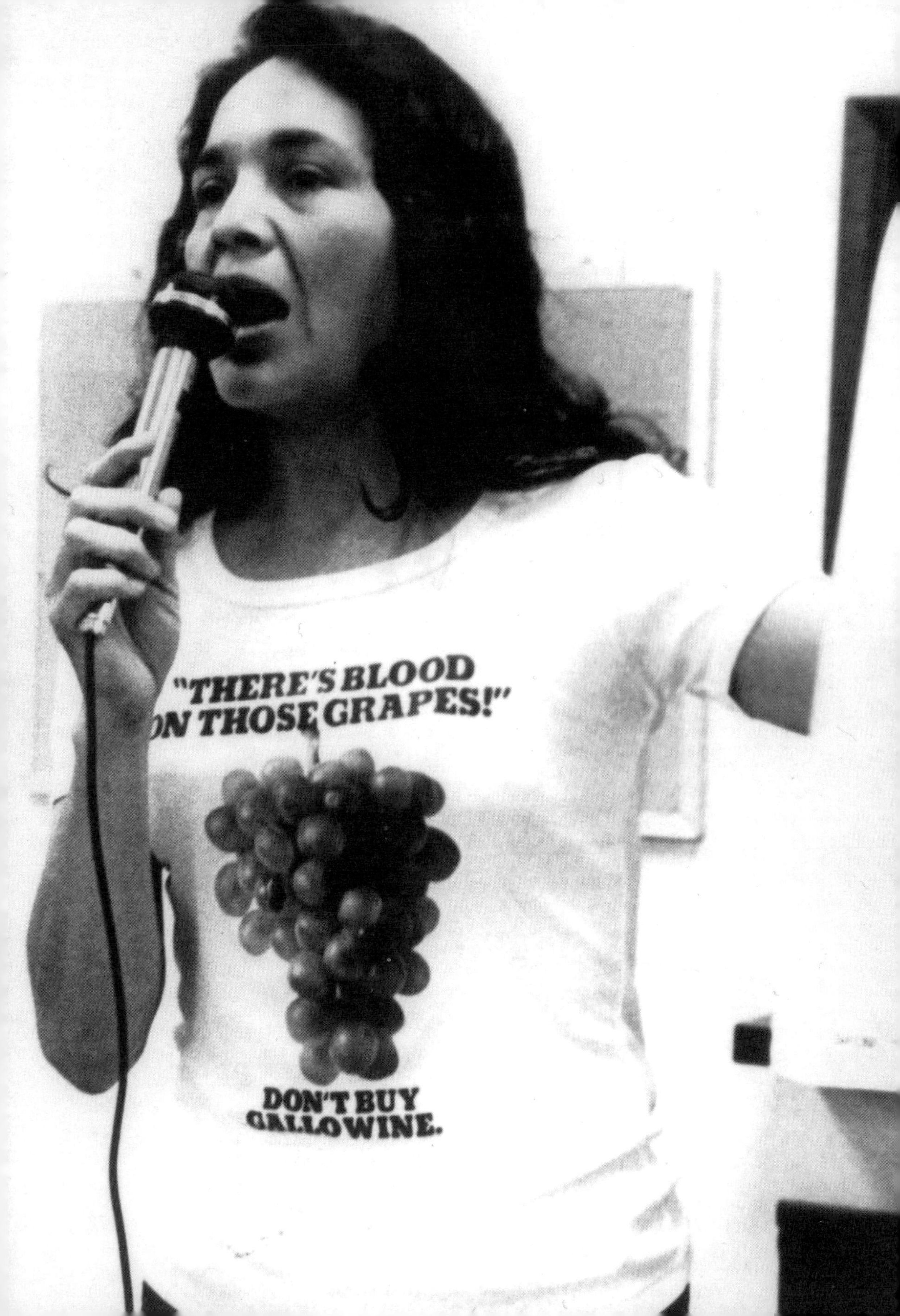
"THERE'S BLOOD
ON THOSE GRAPES!"
DON'T BUY
GALLO WINE.

DOLORES FERNANDEZ HUERTA

[1930–]

*I couldn't stand seeing kids come to class hungry
and needing shoes. I thought I could do more by organizing
farm workers than by trying to teach their hungry children.*

*I don't care what problems we have in this country—they can be
solved by people coming together and organizing.*

—Dolores Huerta

HE NEVER SAW IT COMING! One moment the petite, middle-aged Hispanic woman was distributing papers to a crowd in front of San Francisco's St. Francis Hotel, where Vice President George Bush was speaking. The next minute the woman was lying facedown on the pavement with three broken ribs, a ruptured spleen, and a bleeding gash on her back, the brutal work of a club-wielding police officer.

When Dolores Huerta awoke, she was tucked neatly into a hospital bed. She was informed that she had undergone emergency surgery to remove her spleen, an operation that had been necessary in order to save her life. Huerta also heard that, along with her family and fellow members of the United Farm Workers (UFW), the public was up in arms over the brutality shown by the San Francisco police.

After a full recovery, Huerta, cofounder and vice-president of the UFW, brushed herself off and went right back on the road to continue her life's mission, helping the nation's exploited migrant farm workers and their families. Huerta

---

DOLORES HUERTA *wearing "There's Blood on those Grapes" shirt during the Gallo Strike, c. 1973. Photograph by Cris Sanchez. Courtesy Walter P. Reuther Library, Wayne State University.*

also successfully sued the San Francisco Police Department, an action that resulted in revised methods of crowd control.

As a child growing up in Stockton, California, Huerta was so talkative her grandfather called her "seven tongues." Perhaps the loquacious little girl had recognized at an early age that her words had power, and that one day she would become the "Voice for the Voiceless" and the most famous Mexican American female labor leader in the United States.

The little chatterbox also learned other lessons in childhood that inspired and propelled her through life. From her mother, Dolores learned that a determined, industrious woman could be as successful as a man. Her union-activist father would teach Dolores that the power of an organized group could bring about social change. And from both parents, she learned about her responsibility for helping those in need.

Dolores Fernandez Huerta was born in 1930 during the Great Depression in a small mining town in New Mexico. Her father, Juan Fernandez, was a miner and farm worker, who often toiled twelve to sixteen hours a day picking fruits and vegetables in the hot sun. Frustrated by the pitiful working and living conditions of the migrant workers, he eventually became a union activist and state assemblyman.

When Dolores was three, her parents divorced, and she moved with her mother and two brothers to the city of Stockton in California's San Joaquin Valley. While her mother worked in a canning factory and as a waitress, their grandfather cared for Dolores and her brothers. When her mother had saved enough money, she opened a restaurant, remarried, and bought a seventy-room hotel.

Because the whole family was needed to help in the operation of the businesses, Dolores became aware of the pathetic conditions of the migrant farm workers, who often stayed at the hotel although they were unable to pay. She listened to their stories and complaints about greedy farm owners, and like her father, Dolores became frustrated.

Although Dolores had dreamed of becoming a Spanish dancer, she married her high school sweetheart and had two daughters. When the marriage ended in divorce, she enrolled at a college nearby and earned a teaching degree, with which she hoped to improve the lives of the farm workers in the area.

Most of her students were children of migrant farm workers, who lived in dirt-floor shacks with no running water or indoor toilets. The migrants worked long, hot hours in fields bursting with fruit and vegetables, while many of their own families often went hungry. Dolores also knew that the children were needed at times to work and help support their families, and they would have to miss school. Realizing that she couldn't do anything for these kids who came to

DOLORES HUERTA *marching with The United Farm Workers. Courtesy Walter P. Reuther Library, Wayne State University.*

school barefoot and hungry and often were absent from classes, Dolores began searching for a better way to improve conditions for migrant farm workers.

An opportunity came in 1955, when Dolores was introduced to Fred Ross, the founder of the Mexican American chapter of the Community Service Organization (CSO). The grass roots group had organized voter registration drives, pushed for improved public services and new legislation, and battled everything from police brutality to segregation. Because Ross was not a Hispanic, Dolores was initially skeptical about his sincerity to the cause. But after observing his tireless efforts to improve the Mexican American community by establishing new chapters and offering health clinics, Dolores was convinced that Ross was truly committed to helping migrant workers. She decided to quit teaching and devote her energies and time to improving lives through the CSO.

When her friends and other teachers heard the news, they tried to discourage Dolores from walking away from a job with security and benefits. But Dolores could not be swayed. She was convinced that through the CSO she could actually improve the lives of the exploited farm workers. She focused her energy in learning the techniques of speaking effectively to large gatherings of people and how to win their trust. Soon she was out knocking on doors, encouraging people to register to vote and to attend citizenship classes. She also prodded local government officials to improve the barrios.

While working with the CSO, Dolores met and married her second husband, Ventura Huerta. They had five children together, making Dolores the mother of seven. She adored her children, but Dolores was also passionately dedicated to her work, so she was often away from home, traveling the state to register Mexican American voters.

Her work was always at the forefront of her life, even though she was frequently pregnant during her career. She learned how to combine motherhood and work, changing diapers between meetings, nursing babies during breaks in negotiations, and often taking her children along on the job. Her workaholic ways eventually put a strain on her second marriage, which also ended in divorce. Fortunately, she had the support of her mother, which enabled Dolores to gain custody of her seven children.

Through her work with the CSO, Dolores Huerta developed into an effective speaker and negotiator, and she was sent north to Sacramento to work as a lobbyist at the capitol. While there, she joined the Agricultural Workers Association and met Cesar Chavez, a fellow member of the CSO in California and Arizona. Like Huerta, Chavez was also intensely interested in helping exploited migrant workers.

The CSO campaigned hard to get more Mexican Americans on police forces, in hospitals, and in government offices in the barrios. But Huerta was more concerned about farm workers, a group Chavez believed could be helped only through a union. Fred Ross, who had witnessed the failure of previous efforts to aid the farm workers, did not share their conviction, so Chavez and Huerta left the CSO to devote their combined energies to their mission.

The National Farm Workers Association (NFWA) was established in 1962, with the word "union" omitted because of its possible negative effect. After Chavez was named president and Huerta vice-president, the two officers launched a campaign to organize migrant farm workers. Huerta moved her children to Delano, California, to join the Chavez family and to begin her work at the newly founded NFWA headquarters. Although it was a time when most Mexican Americans believed strongly that a woman's place was in the home, Huerta refused to let these attitudes distract her from working to build the union. She concentrated on the goals of NFWA: to create a union in order to bargain effectively with produce growers; to secure better wages, better living conditions, and a safer work environment for the migrant farm workers; and to operate in a nonviolent manner.

The union workers bonded together like a large extended family, a situation that allowed Huerta to concentrate on gathering funds for the union's survival. Dues were set at $3.50 per month, a large sum for the low-paid farm workers. Huerta covered northern California and Cesar worked the southern part, driving from town to town, holding organizational meetings, and explaining how each member bought a voice in the NFWA with their dues.

The relentless campaign to sign up new members in the union, make speeches, and negotiate contracts, won Huerta an international reputation as a speaker and politician. Her persuasive lobbying efforts helped secure aid for dependent families and disability insurance for California farm workers in 1963. The traveling, hard work, and long hours finally began to pay off two years later when the union reported a membership of twelve hundred families, all enjoying community service programs, life insurance, and a credit union.

The first union protest occurred in 1965, when a group of migrant workers at a rose farm complained they were paid less then originally promised by the nursery owner. Chavez and Huerta advised the union workers to stay home from work until the owner paid them what he had originally promised. Some of the migrant workers were frightened and talked about going back to work, but Huerta blocked their cars with her truck. After four days, the farm owner agreed to the demands of the workers and paid the promised amount.

After this first NFWA victory, confidence in union power grew. A few months later Filipino grape pickers, members of the Agricultural Workers Organizing Committee, decided to strike a California vineyard. When they asked NFWA for help, the members voted to join the strike, and Huerta began working on a strategy that soon captured the attention of the entire country.

The famous Delano Grape Strike began as a three-hundred-mile march, extending from the union's main office in Delano to the state capitol building in Sacramento. Seventy marchers protested peacefully, carrying posters and banners, but growers still refused to recognize the union. Huerta decided to use another tactic, the boycott.

In the winter of 1967–68, Huerta took a group of farm workers to New York, the primary distribution point for grapes, to organize a grape boycott there. She stayed for two years, leading marches and rallies in area cities and towns as millions of people accompanied the farm workers on their marches to show their support. Huerta's powerful speeches brought in new supporters, including the government, who agreed to support the boycott and refrain from buying California grapes, but the strike and boycott dragged on.

Union membership continued to grow as Huerta negotiated a contract with the powerful Schenley Wine Company. It was the first time in U.S. history that

CESAR CHAVEZ *in front of UFW symbol. Courtesy Walter P. Reuther Library, Wayne State University.*

farm workers would negotiate a collective bargaining agreement with an agricultural corporation. As the union's main negotiator, Huerta created contracts that established working conditions and benefit plans for farm workers until the strike was finally settled.

Cesar Chavez, in the meantime, decided to stir the waters by staging a nonviolent protest like the one used by Mohandas K. Gandhi in 1947 to help gain India's independence from Great Britain. To draw attention to the cause, Chavez fasted for twenty-five days, eating nothing and losing thirty-five pounds, while the national media reported the details to a sympathetic nation.

The Delano Grape Strike involved more than five thousand grape workers who walked off their jobs for a strike that would last for five years. Finally, in 1970, a contract was signed to benefit all farm workers, one that raised the minimum wage and added paid holidays and vacations. The lengthy strike was a major victory for the NFWA and cause for celebration. Huerta, who personally wrote, negotiated, and administered the agreements, was finally free to return to her children.

By 1970 most of the vineyards were paying fair wages, and NFWA was at its peak with more than seventy thousand members. In 1972, a merger between NFWA and the AFL-CIO resulted in the most powerful labor union in the country, the United Farm Workers of America. Cesar Chavez was elected president and Dolores Huerta, vice-president.

When Dolores married her third husband, Richard Chavez, Cesar's brother, she finally gained a soul mate, a man who shared her passion for the union, and who did not resent the time she gave to the cause. They produced four children together.

Huerta's inspiring speeches, nonviolent landmark boycotts, and successful negotiating skills won the support of such diverse groups as feminists, peace groups, religious organizations, Hispanic associations, and student protesters. With her forceful and uncompromising manner, Huerta was instrumental in gaining passage of the 1975 Agricultural Labor Relations Act of California, the first bill of rights for farm workers ever enacted in America. In 1980 she cofounded KUFW Radio Campesina, the UFW's radio station in California. She often testifies before state and federal committees on issues that effect migrant farm workers.

Although Huerta has always supported the union's nonviolent philosophy, her own life has often been in danger. Arrested more than twenty times, she suffered serious injury from police brutality in 1988 during a peaceful demonstration in San Francisco. Huerta was rushed to the hospital with broken ribs and a ruptured spleen, which was removed during emergency surgery. The media attention and public outrage over the incident resulted in a revision of the San Francisco Police Department's crowd-control tactics.

When her great friend and UFW cofounder Cesar Chavez died at the age of sixty-six in 1993, Huerta promised that their struggle would go on. The woman Chavez once described as "totally fearless, both mentally and physically" remains as passionate to La Causa as ever, still committed to justice, dignity, and a decent standard of living for migrant farm workers. "I think we brought to the world the whole idea of boycotting as a nonviolent tactic. I think we showed the world that nonviolence can work to make social change."

Huerta's accomplishments have made her the most prominent Chicana labor leader in the entire United States and the recipient of many prestigious awards, including the Eleanor Roosevelt Award for Human Rights, presented to Huerta by President Clinton in 1999. She has become a role model for Mexican American women, who admire her support for women in positions of power. They also know that Huerta, who was often pregnant during her career, understands the difficulties of working mothers.

Still incredibly energetic, this mother of eleven children, grandmother of fourteen, and great-grandmother of four, continues her nonviolent struggle for the rights of the migrant farm workers. Retirement may not be an option for Dolores Fernandez Huerta Chavez, who says, "I'll just keep going as long as I can, and die with my boots on."

SANDRA DAY O'CONNOR

[1930–]

The first female member of the U.S. Supreme Court
is known for her sharp mind and conservative views.
But few people are aware that the esteemed justice is as competent
in the saddle as she is on the bench.
Raised on an Arizona cattle ranch, Sandra Day O'Connor
could ride, shoot, brand cattle, mend fences, and drive a truck
before she was ten years old.

O N THE PACKED COURTROOM on the afternoon of September 25, 1981, all eyes were glued to the two doors at the front of the room. When they finally opened, President Ronald Reagan walked into the room from one side. From the other door, Sandra Day O'Connor entered, ready to be sworn in as the first female member of the United States Supreme Court.

After solemnly swearing to support and defend the Constitution of the United States, O'Connor put on the black robe of a Supreme Court Justice and walked to the far end of the bench. That moment, when she joined the eight black-robed men on the nation's highest court, O'Connor made history and shattered a tradition that had been in existence for 191 years.

O'Connor's position as the lone woman in a group of men was not an unfamiliar role for the former cowgirl, who spent her childhood working alongside cowboys on her family's Arizona cattle ranch. Chores had no gender on the Lazy B, so O'Connor grew up sharing duties with the ranch hands and became a competent cowgirl in the process. Years later, far from the Lazy B, O'Connor

SANDRA DAY O'CONNOR *portrait in 1970. Photograph by Markow Photography, Phoenix, Arizona. Courtesy The Supreme Court of the United States Office of the Curator.*

continued to blaze trails in male-dominated areas and reach places no woman before her had ever been.

Sandra Day was born in El Paso, Texas, in 1930, the eldest of Harry and Ada Mae Day's three children. She spent her childhood on the family's Lazy B Ranch, which sprawled across 198,000 acres in southeastern Arizona along the border of New Mexico. Her grandfather had established the ranch back in 1880, when Arizona was still a territory, and Sandra knew every dusty mile of it.

Sandra grew up during the Depression years, when life for the Day family was rugged and hard. The Lazy B had no running water or electricity, and the closest town was twenty-five miles away. But Sandra didn't care. She knew the names of the horses in the stable and thrilled at the sight of the huge herd of cattle that roamed the arid acres of the Lazy B. Her best friends were her pet bobcat, a pair of javelinas, and the ranch hands, the men who helped Sandra become a competent cowgirl. By the time she was ten years old, there was little on the ranch that Sandra couldn't fix or do. She could ride like the wind, brand cattle, mend a broken fence, make adobe bricks, shoot a rifle, and drive a truck.

Along with hard work, education was very important in the Day family. So, when Sandra reached school age, her parents sent her to El Paso, Texas, to live with her maternal grandmother and attend a private girl's school there. Once the school year was over, Sandra eagerly returned to the ranch where she spent the summer. A few months later, when it was time to return to school in El Paso, Sandra became heartsick.

Although Sandra loved her grandmother and enjoyed living in the comfortable El Paso home, with its fancy electric lights and faucets that poured warm water, she loved the Lazy B even more and missed it greatly. At her grandmother's, Sandra learned the importance of homework and of being prepared and setting high goals for herself. The lessons learned on the ranch and those instilled by her grandmother would help propel Sandra through an impressive career and eventually to the top spot in her profession.

A quiet, introverted student, Sandra often suffered bouts of homesickness for the Lazy B. To ease the pain, she focused her energies on her studies, and graduated from high school at age sixteen. She enrolled at Stanford University, majoring in economics, and graduated cum laude in 1950. Although she planned to return to ranch life, Sandra changed her mind when she learned of a legal dispute involving the Lazy B. She enrolled in Stanford Law School and received the LL.B. two years later, ranking third out of 102 students.

During her years at Stanford, Sandra was editor of the *Stanford Law Review*, a position that brought her in contact with two men who greatly influenced her life. One was her coeditor and fellow classmate, William H. Rehnquist, the future Chief Justice of the Supreme Court. The other was a law student named John Jay O'Connor III, whose sense of humor won the heart of the serious Sandra Day. They married in 1952, six months after Sandra's graduation, in a wedding ceremony at the Lazy B Ranch.

Although she was highly qualified for a job as a lawyer, Sandra Day O'Connor soon discovered that work in the real world was not so gender-free as in ranch life. It was the early 1950s, and law firms were not interested in hiring female lawyers. One firm that did show an interest in O'Connor was located in Los Angeles, and the position they offered O'Connor was for legal secretary. Although she turned down the offer, thirty years later, one of the firm's partners, William French Smith, then the United States Attorney General, advised President Reagan to appoint O'Connor to the Supreme Court.

The public service sector proved to be more accepting of women, so O'Connor refocused her job search and found a position as deputy county attorney for San Mateo, California. It was a job that O'Connor would claim "influenced the balance of my life because it demonstrated how much I did enjoy public service." Although she enjoyed the work, she left a year later to join her husband, who had been drafted into the army and sent to Frankfurt, Germany. During the couple's three years in Europe, Sandra O'Connor worked as a civilian lawyer in the U.S. Army Quartermaster's Corps.

In 1957 her husband's tour of duty was over, so the O'Connors returned to the U.S. and moved to Phoenix, Arizona, where they built a home and started a family. Within the next six years, Sandra gave birth to three sons. She also opened a law firm with a partner, where she worked part time, hoping to develop a specialization and build a reputation. After the birth of her second son, O'Connor took a five-year leave to care for her children on a full-time basis.

Energetic and well-organized, O'Connor combined motherhood with volunteer activities and civic affairs. She became involved with the Arizona State Hospital, the Arizona State Bar, Salvation Army, the Maricopa County Board of Adjustments and Appeals, and the Governor's Committee on Marriage and Family. She acted as court referee in juvenile cases, started a legal referral service for the county bar, and joined the Arizona Republican Party, serving as district chair. In 1965, five years after she left professional life, the intelligent, diplomatic O'Connor had established a sound family foundation, impressive legal credentials, and good connections. It also didn't hurt that she was detailed, industrious, intelligent, and attractive. About that time in her life, O'Connor would say, "Two things were clear to me from the onset. One is, I wanted a family and the second was that I wanted to work—and I love to work."

Being sworn in as associate Supreme Court Justice in 1981. Photograph by Michael Evans, The White House. Courtesy The Supreme Court of the United States Office of the Curator.

O'Connor reentered professional life as Arizona's assistant attorney general, a position she held until 1969, when she was appointed to fill a vacant Arizona senate seat. A well-known Republican, O'Connor defended her seat and easily won election in 1970 and again in 1972. Her years in the state senate were marked with diplomacy, fastidious attention to detail, and the ability to get things done. When her fellow Republicans chose her the party's majority leader in 1972, she became the first woman in the country to ever hold the post.

A moderate to conservative legislator, O'Connor voted for government spending limits and the death penalty. She supported the Equal Rights Amendment and voted for better property rights for women. She refused to be pinned down on the subject of abortion, and voted to repeal state laws making abortion illegal. Later she voted to limit access to and restrict state funding for abortions, and for the right of refusal to perform abortions.

Even though she was a successful state senator, O'Connor never seemed comfortable in the political setting. In 1974, she changed the course of her career with a move that set the stage for her climb to the highest court in the land. Although many of O'Connor's supporters felt it was a step down, O'Connor ran for the judgeship of the Maricopa County Superior Court. After a hard fight, O'Connor won the election and went on to build a reputation as a tough but fair-minded judge, who suffered no qualms about imposing the death penalty when she saw fit.

O'Connor remained an active member of the Republican Party and served as alternate delegate to the 1972 Republican National Convention. She cochaired Richard Nixon's reelection committee in Arizona, and four years later backed Ronald Reagan in his unsuccessful attempt to wrench the nomination from President Gerald Ford. In 1978, party leaders encouraged O'Connor to run for governor, but she declined.

With her career and reputation prospering, O'Connor was appointed to Arizona's Court of Appeals. A few years later, President Reagan began searching the country for the right woman to appoint to the Supreme Court, to fill a seat being vacated by retiring Justice Potter Steward. By appointing a woman, the President hoped to fulfill the pledge he made to the women's movement to counterbalance his earlier opposition to the Equal Rights Amendment. He had been reminded at the time that no woman had ever served on the Supreme Court, and the President wanted to correct the situation. But whom would he appoint?

After interviewing O'Connor personally and studying her credentials, the President called off the search. He knew that he had found the right woman for the job. Reporters, responding to rumors of the decision, hounded O'Connor about the possibility of the historic nomination, but she politely refused to comment. The media buzzed with speculation until President Reagan called for a televised press conference and announced his pledge to appoint a woman who met the very high standards of Supreme Court appointees. He then introduced Sandra Day O'Connor, a "person for all seasons," who possessed the "qualities of temperament, fairness, intellectual capacity, and devotion to the public good."

Along with the attributes mentioned by the President, O'Connor had the proper conservative credentials, was an old friend of the Chief Justice, and was able to rally widespread support. With her historic nomination as the first woman nominated to the high court, O'Connor received a barrage of criticism from the left and right. Accusations ranged from her inexperience in federal and constitutional knowledge to claims that her position was enhanced by her political connections with her old Stanford classmate, Chief Justice Rehnquist. The Christian right was also outraged, calling her nomination a "disaster" and a "betrayal" of their cause.

However, the Senate Judiciary Committee voted unanimously for her confirmation, and on September 26, 1981, Sandra Day O'Connor was sworn in as the

JUSTICE SANDRA DAY O'CONNOR, *Associate Justice, Supreme Court of the United States. Photograph by Dane Penland, Smithsonian Institution. Courtesy The Supreme Court of the United States Office of the Curator.*

102nd member of the United States Supreme Court. Her nomination was hailed by senators across the political spectrum, and applauded by feminists who counted on her support for women's issues. O'Connor, the law school graduate who couldn't find a job in 1952 as a lawyer because she was a woman, had just been appointed to the Supreme Court for the same reason in 1981.

As the country's first female Supreme Court Justice, O'Connor became an instant celebrity. She appeared in society pages of Washington newspapers, and rumors floated around that she might be the Republican's choice for a vice-presidential candidate. After her husband moved his law practice to Washington, the O'Connors became part of the social whirl there. Shortly after taking her seat on the court, O'Connor organized an exercise class in the former all-male gym for woman employees. She also received many requests to speak, but O'Connor avoided the lecture circuit and shunned media attention.

All the hoopla over her position as the court's first and only woman settled down when O'Connor proceeded to behave on the court like any conservative male justice. Her strong support for states' rights classified O'Connor a conservative, but she proved to vary her views on other issues and establish a unique voice on the court. She later explained that "the power I exert on the court depends on the power of my arguments, not on my gender."

By her second year on the court, O'Connor's appeal to the feminists began to wane. She disappointed them when she refused to allow her decision favoring women's equity with men to become retroactive, and she frustrated pro-choice advocates by voting to curb access to abortion. Through the years, O'Connor has been called a "traitor" by liberals for her compromise on abortion rights, although later many appreciated her efforts to keep the Roe v. Wade Decision intact. If feminists have not always agreed with her decisions, O'Connor has proved herself an excellent role model for women in general.

Her courage was apparent in 1988, when doctors diagnosed O'Connor with breast cancer. Remaining true to her nature, she methodically researched the disease before agreeing to a mastectomy. The day before surgery she kept her speaking date at Washington and Lee University, and ten days later, after her surgery, she said, "the prognosis is for total recovery. I do not anticipate missing any oral arguments." With stamina intact, O'Connor was back in court five days after her release from the hospital.

During her decades on the court, O'Connor has become a more confident and independent justice. A tough taskmaster, she strives to give each case individual treatment and reach a practical conclusion, and often holds the deciding "swing" vote on an evenly divided court. Although her conservatism once concerned activists, her court record has been moderate. With her varied professional background and unique, thoughtful voice, O'Connor ranks as one of the best-respected members of the court.

O'Connor's "lone woman" status on the court ended in 1993, when Ruth Bader Ginsburg became the second female member of the Supreme Court. No longer a male bastion, the Supreme Court today is open to women and men, who share a gender-free workload, like the chores Sandra Day O'Connor once shared with the cowboys on the Lazy B.

BIBLIOGRAPHY

INTRODUCTION

Armitage, Susan and Elizabeth Jameson. *The Women's West*. Norman: University of Oklahoma Press, 1987.

Brown, Dee Alexander. *The Westerners*. New York: Holt, Rinehart, and Winston, 1974.

Duncan, Dayton and Ken Burns. *Lewis and Clark: The Journey of the Corps of Discovery*. New York: Alfred A. Knopf, 1999.

Greenspan, Karen. *The Timetables of Women's History: A Chronology of the Most Important People and Events in Women's History*. New York: Simon & Schuster, 1994.

Heinemann, Sue. *Timelines of American Women's History*. New York: Berkley Publishing Group, 1996.

Jameson, Elizabeth and Susan Armitage. *Writing The Range: Race, Class, and Culture in the Women's West*. Norman: University of Oklahoma Press, 1997.

Milner, Clyde II, Carol O'Connor, and Martha Sandweiss. *The Oxford History of the American West*. New York: Oxford University Press, 1994.

Read, Phyllis J. and Bernard L. Witlieb. *The Book of Women's Firsts*. New York: Random House, 1992.

Sanford, Trent Elwood. *The Architecture of the Southwest*. Tucson: University of Arizona Press, 1978

Schlissel, Lilliian. *Women's Diaries of the Westward Journey*. New York: Schocken Books, 1982.

Schlissel, Lillian, and Catherine Lavender. *The Western Women's Reader*. New York: Harper Collins, 2000.

Sicherman, Barbara and Carol Hurd Green. *Notable American Women: The Modern Period*. Cambridge, MA: Radcliffe College, Belknap Press of Harvard University Press, 1980.

Summerhayes, Martha. *Vanished Arizona: Recollections of the Army Life of a New England Woman*. Glorieta, NM: Rio Grande Press, 1908.

Trimble, Marshall. *Arizona: A Cavalcade of History*. Tucson: Treasure Chest Publications, 1989.

———. *Roadside History of Arizona*. Missoula, MT: Mountain Press Publishing Company, 1986.

Weatherford, Doris. *American Women's History*. New York: Prentice Hall General Reference, 1994.

Weglyn, Michi Nishiura. *Years of Infamy: The Untold Story of America's Concentration Camps*. Seattle: University of Washington Press, 1996.

SACAGAWEA

Ambrose, Stephen E. *Undaunted Courage: Meriwether Lewis, Thomas Jefferson, and the Opening of the American West*. New York: Touchstone-Simon & Shuster, 1996.

Ashby, Ruth and Deborah Ohrn. *Herstory: Women Who Changed the World*. New York: Viking, 1995.

Brown, Dee Alexander. *The Westerners*. New York: Holt, Rinehart, and Winston, 1974.

Duncan, Dayton and Ken Burns. *Lewis and Clark: The Journey of the Corps of Discovery*. New York: Alfred A. Knopf, 1999.

Ferris, Robert, ed. *Lewis and Clark*. Washington, D.C.: United States Department of the Interior, National Park Service, 1975.

Forbes, Malcolm. *Women Who Made a Difference*. New York: Simon and Schuster, 1990.

Gilbert, Bill. *The Trailblazers*. New York: Time-Life Books, 1973.

Holloway, David. *Lewis and Clark and the Crossing of North America*. New York: Saturday Review Press, 1974.

Milner, Clyde II, Carol O'Connor, and Martha Sandweiss. *The Oxford History of the American West*. New York: Oxford University Press, 1994.

Thomasma, Kenneth. *The Truth About Sacajawea*. Jackson, WY: Grandview Publishing Company, 1997.

Uglow, Jennifer S. *The Continuum Dictionary of Women's Biography*. New York: Continuum Publishing Company, 1982.

ESTHER HOBART SLACK MORRIS

Armitage, Susan and Elizabeth Jameson. *The Women's West* . Norman: University of Oklahoma Press, 1987.

Brown, Dee. *The Gentle Tamers: Women of the Old Wild West*. Lincoln: University of Nebraska Press, 1958.

Frost, Elizabeth and Kathryn Cullen-DuPont. *Women's Suffrage in America: An Eyewitness History*. New York: Facts on File, 1992.

Levenson, Dorothy. *Women of the West*. Franklin Watts, 1973.

BRIDGET BIDDY MASON

Hull, LeAnne von Neumeye. "A Story of Bridget 'Biddy' Smith Mason: Her Legacy Among the Mormons." www.ldssocal.org/history/biddymason.htm.

Katz, William Loren. *Black People Who Made the Old West*. New York: Thomas Y. Crowell Company, 1977.

Levy, JoAnn. *They Saw the Elephant: Women and the California Goldrush*. Hamden, CT: Archon Books (The Shoe String Press), 1990.

Pelz, Ruth. *Women of the Wild West*. Seattle: Open Hand Publishing Company, 1995.

Robinson, Deidre. *Open Hands, Open Heart: The Story of Biddy Mason*. Gardena, CA: Sly Fox Publishing Company, 1998.

Sherr, Lynn and Jurate Kazickas. *Susan B. Anthony Slept Here: A Guide to American Women's Landmarks*. New York: Random House, 1994.

Smith, Jessie Carney. *Epic Lives: One Hundred Black Women Who Made a Difference*. Washington, D.C.: Visible Ink Press, 1993.

Wheeler, B. Gordon. *Black California: The History of African-Americans in the Golden State*. New York: Hippocrene Books, 1993.

ABIGAIL SCOTT DUNIWAY

Forbes, Malcolm. *Women Who Made a Difference*. New York: Simon & Schuster, 1990.

Frost, Elizabeth and Kathryn Cullen-DuPont. *Women's Suffrage in America: An Eyewitness History*. New York: Facts on File, 1992.

Greenspan, Karen. *The Timetables of Women's History: A Chronology of the Most Important People and Events in Women's History*. New York: Simon & Schuster, 1994.

Moynihan, Ruth Barnes. *Rebel For Rights: Abigail Scott Duniway*. New Haven, CT: Yale University Press, 1983.

Riley, Glenda and Richard Etulain. *By Grit and Grace: Eleven Women Who Shaped the American West*. Golden, CO: Fulcrum Publishing, 1997.

Seagraves, Anne. *Daughters of the West*. Hayden, ID: Wesanne Publications, 1996.

Wheeler, Marjorie Spruill. *One Woman, One Vote: Rediscovering the Woman Suffrage Movement*. Troutdale, OR: NewSage Press, 1995.

NELLIE CASHMAN

Banks, Leo W. *Stalwart Women: Frontier Stories of Indomitable Spirit*. Phoenix: Arizona Highways Books, 1999.

Chaput, Don. *Nellie Cashman and the North American Mining Frontier*. Tucson: Westernlore Press, 1995.

Clum, John P. "Nellie Cashman: The Angel of Tombstone". Tucson: *Arizona Historical Review*, January 1931.

Ledbetter, Susan. *Nellie Cashman: Prospector and Trailblazer*. El Paso: Texas Western Press, 1993.

Seagraves, Anne. *High Spirited Women of the West*. Hayden, ID: Wesanne Publications, 1992.

Trimble, Marshall. *Arizona: A Cavalcade of History*. Tucson: Treasure Chest Publications, 1990.

Zanjani, Sally. *A Mine of Her Own: Women Prospectors in the American West, 1850–1950*. Lincoln: University of Nebraska Press, 1997.

SARAH WINNEMUCCA

Ashby, Ruth and Deborah Ohrn. *Herstory: Women Who Changed the World*. New York: Viking, 1995.

Canfield, Gae Whitney. *Sarah Winnemucca of the Northern Paiutes*. Norman: University of Oklahoma Press, 1983.

Heinemann, Sue. *Timelines of American Women's History*. New York: Berkley Publishing Group, 1996.

Hopkins, Sara Winnemucca. *Life Among the Piutes: Their Wrongs and Claims*. Edited by Mrs. Horace Mann. Boston and New York: privately printed, 1883. Reprint, Bishop, California: Chalfant Press, 1969.

Richey, Elinor. *Eminent Women of the West*. Berkeley, CA: Howell-North Books, 1975

Seagraves, Anne. *High-Spirited Women of the West*. Hayden, ID: Wesanne Publications, 1992.

LOTTA CRABTREE

Johnson, William Weber. *The Forty-Niners*. New York: Time-Life Books, 1974.

Levy, JoAnn. *They Saw the Elephant: Women and the California Goldrush*. Hamden, CT: Archon Books/The Shoe String Press, 1990.

Seagraves, Anne. *Women of the Sierra*. Hayden, ID: Wesanne Publications, 1990.

Riley, Glenda and Richard Etulain. *By Grit and Grace: Eleven Women Who Shaped the American West*. Golden, CO: Fulcrum Publishing, 1997.

Weatherford, Doris. *American Women's History*. New York: Prentice Hall General Reference, 1994.

MARTHA HUGHES CANNON

Bartholomew, Rebecca. *Audacious Women: Early British Mormon Immigrants*. Salt Lake City: Signature Books, 1995.

Heinemann, Sue. *Timelines of American Women's History*. New York: Berkley Publishing Group, 1996.

Leiber, Constance L. and John Sillito. *Letters from Exile: The Correspondence of Martha Hughes Cannon and Angus M. Cannon, 1886–1888*. Salt Lake City: Signature Books, 1989.

Slaughter, William W. *Life in Zion: An Intimate Look at the Latter Day Saints, 1820–1995*. Salt Lake City: Deseret Book Company, 1995.

Van Wagoner, Richard S. *Mormon Polygamy: A History*. Salt Lake City: Signature Books, 1989.

MAY ARKWRIGHT HUTTON

Cheney, Roberta. *The Women Who Made the West*. New York: Doubleday & Company, 1980.

Hutton, May Arkwright. *The Coeur D'Alenes or A Tale of the Modern Inquisition in Idaho*. Fairfield, WA: Ye Galleon Press, 1900.

Montgomery, James W. *Liberated Woman: A Life of May Arkwright Hutton*. Spokane: Gingko House Publishers, 1974.

Pelz, Ruth. *Women of the Wild West*. Seattle: Open Hand Publishing, 1995.

MARY HUNTER AUSTIN

Austin, Mary. *The Land of Little Rain*. Albuquerque: University of New Mexico Press, 1974.

———. *Earth Horizon, An Autobiography*. Albuquerque: University of New Mexico Press, 1932.

Finch, Robert and John Elder. *The Norton Book of Nature Writing*. New York: W. W. Norton & Company, 1990.

Fink, Augusta. *I-Mary: A Biography of Mary Austin*. Tucson: University of Arizona Press, 1983.

Heinemann, Sue. *Timelines of American Women's History*. New York: Berkley Publishing Group, 1996.

Lyon, Thomas J. *The Literary West: An Anthology of Western American Literature*. New York: Oxford University Press, 1999.

Schlissel, Lillian, and Catherine Lavender. *The Western Women's Reader*. New York: Harper Collins, 2000.

Stineman, Esther Lanigan. *Mary Austin: Song of a Maverick*. New Haven, CT: Yale University Press, 1989.

Work, James C. *Prose and Poetry Of The American West*. Norman: University of Nebraska Press, 1990.

MARY ELIZABETH JANE COLTER

Anderson, Michael F. *Living At the Edge: Explorers, Exploiters, and Settlers of the Grand Canyon Region*. Grand Canyon: Grand Canyon Association, 1998.

Bleiberg, Larry. "Grand Design: Architect Mary Colter's Buildings Help Define the Grand Canyon." *Dallas Morning News,* May 24, 1998.

Ford, Susan Jezak. *Mary Elizabeth Colter: Architect and Designer*. Kansas City, MO: Kansas City Public Library.

Grattan, Virginia L. *Mary Colter: Builder Upon the Red Earth*. Grand Canyon: Grand Canyon Natural History Association, 1992.

Poling-Kempes, Lesley. *The Harvey Girls: Women Who Opened the West*. New York: Marlowe & Company, 1989.

NELLIE TAYLOE ROSS

American Heritage Center. *Nellie Tayloe Ross Papers.* Laramie: University of Wyoming, 1998.

Hallberg, Carl. *Women's History in Wyoming.* Cheyenne: Wyoming State Archives, 2000.

Weatherford, Doris. *American Women's History.* New York: Prentice Hall General Reference, 1994.

JEANNETTE PICKERING RANKIN

Frost, Elizabeth and Kathryn Cullen-DuPont. *Women's Suffrage in America: An Eyewitness History.* New York: Facts on File, 1992.

Heinemann, Sue. *Timelines of American Women's History.* New York: Berkley Publishing Group, 1996.

Josephson, Hannah. *Jeannette Rankin: First Lady in Congress.* Indianapolis, IN: Bobbs-Merrill Company, Inc., 1974.

Read, Phyllis J. and Bernard L. Witlieb. *The Book of Women's Firsts.* New York: Random House, 1992.

Seagraves, Anne. *Daughters of the West.* Hayden, ID: Wesanne Publications, 1996.

Uglow, Jennifer S. *The Continuum Dictionary of Women's Biography.* New York: Continuum Publishing Company, 1982.

Wheeler, Marjorie Spruill. *One Woman, One Vote: Rediscovering the Woman Suffrage Movement.* Troutman, OR: NewSage Press, 1995.

GEORGIA O'KEEFFE

Ashby, Ruth and Deborah Gore Ohrn. *Herstory: Women Who Changed the World.* New York: Viking, 1995.

Berry, Michael. *Georgia O'Keeffe.* New York: Chelsea House Publishers, 1988.

Eldredge, Charles C. *Georgia O'Keeffe.* New York: Harry N. Abrams, 1991.

Gherman, Beverly. *Georgia O'Keeffe: The Wideness and Wonder of Her World.* New York: Atheneum, 1986.

Hassrick, Peter H., ed. *The Georgia O'Keeffe Museum.* New York: Harry N. Abrams, 1997.

Poling, John D. *Painting with O'Keeffe.* Lubbock: Texas Tech University Press, 1999.

Raven, Susan and Alison Weir. *Women of Achievement: Thirty-Five Centuries of History.* New York: Harmony Books, 1981.

MARY PICKFORD

Acker, Ally. *Reel Women: Pioneers of the Cinema, 1896 to the Present.* New York: Continuum Publishing Company, 1991.

Brownlow, Kevin. *Mary Pickford Rediscovered.* New York: Henry N. Abrams, in association with the Academy of Motion Picture Arts and Sciences, 1999.

Heinemann, Sue. *Timelines of American Women's History.* New York: Berkley Publishing Group, 1996.

Raven, Susan and Alison Weir. *Women of Achievement: Thirty-Five Centuries of History.* New York: Harmony Books, 1981.

Slide, Anthony. *Early American Cinema.* Metuchen, NJ: Scarecrow Press, 1994.

Sova, Dawn B. *Women in Hollywood: From Vamp to Studio Head.* New York: Fromm International Publishing, 1988.

Weatherford, Doris. *American Women's History.* New York: Prentice Hall General Reference, 1994.

Whitfield, Eileen. *Pickford: The Woman Who Made Hollywood.* Lexington: The University of Kentucky, 1997.

Uglow, Jennifer S. *The Continuum Dictionary of Women's Biography.* New York: Continuum Publishing Company, 1982.

DOROTHEA LANGE

Felder, Deborah G. *The 100 Most Influential Women of All Time.* Secaucus, NJ: Carol Publishing Group, 1996.

Foner, Eric and John A. Garraty, eds. *The Readers Companion to American History.* Boston: Houghton Mifflin Company, 1991.

Partridge, Elizabeth. *Restless Spirit: The Life and Work of Dorothea Lange.* New York: Viking, 1998.

JACQUELINE COCHRAN

Cochran, Jacqueline and Floyd Odlum. *The Stars at Noon.* Boston: Little, Brown and Company, 1974.

Cochran, Jacqueline and Maryann Bucknam Brinley. *Jackie Cochran, An Autobiography.* New York: Bantam Books, 1987.

Felder, Deborah G. *A Century of Women, The Most Influential Events in Twentieth-Century Women's History.* Secaucus, NJ: Carol Publishing Group, 1999.

Haynsworth, Leslie and Toomey, David. *Amelia Earhart's Daughters, The Wild and Glorious Story of American Women Aviators from Wrold War II to the Dawn of the Space Age.* New York: William Morrow and Company, Inc., 1998.

Jaros, Dean. *Heroes Without Legacy; American Airwomen, 1912–1944,* Nowot: University Press of Colorado, 1993.

Lomax, Judy, *Women of the Air.* New York: Dodd, Mead & Company, 1987.

McGuire, Nina and Sandra Wallus Sammons. *Jacqueline Cochran: America's Fearless Aviator.* Lake Buena Vista, FL: Southern Pioneer Press, 1997.

Moolman, Valerie. *Women Aloft.* Alexandria, VA: Time-Life Books, 1981.

Read, Phyllis J. and Bernard L. Witlieb. *The Book of Women's Firsts.* New York: Random House, 1992.

MILDRED BABE DIDRIKSON ZAHARIAS

Ashby, Ruth and Deborah Ohrn. *Herstory: Women Who Changed the World.* New York: Viking, 1995.

Freedman, Russell. *Babe Didrikson Zaharias: The Making of a Champion.* New York: Clarion Books, 1999.

Garber, Angus G., III. *Golf Legends: Players, Holes, Life on the Tours.* New York: Gallery Books, 1988.

Glenn, Rhonda. *Illustrated History of Women's Golf.* Dallas: Taylor Publishing Company, 1991.

Hahn, James and Lynn Hahn. *Zaharias!: The Sports Career of Mildred Zaharias.* Mankato, MN: Crestwood House, 1981.

Knudson, R. R. *Babe Didrikson: Athlete of the Century.* New York: Viking Penguin, 1985.

Lynn, Elizabeth A. *Babe Didrikson Zaharias: Champion Athlete.* New York: Chelsea House Publishers, 1989.

Nickerson, Elinor. *Golf: A Women's History.* Jefferson, NC: McFarland & Company, 1987.

Schoor, Gene. *Babe Didrikson: The World's Greatest Woman Athlete.* New York: Doubleday & Company, 1978.

Uglow, Jennifer S. *The Continuum Dictionary of Women's Biography.* New York: Continuum Publishing Company, 1982.

DOLORES FERNANDEZ HUERTA

Heinemann, Sue. *Timelines of American Women's History.* New York: Berkley Publishing Group, 1996.

Holmes, Burnham. *Cesar Chavez: Farm Worker Activist.* Austin, TX: Raintree Steck-Vaughn, 1994.

Kanellos, Nicholas, ed. *The Hispanic-American Almanac: A Reference Work on Hispanics in the United States.* Detroit: Gale Research, 1993.

Morey, Janet. *Famous Mexican Americans.* New York: Dutton, 1989.

Perez, Frank. *Dolores Huerta.* Austin, TX: Raintree Steck-Vaughn Publishers, 1996.

SANDRA DAY O'CONNOR

Berry, Dawn Bradley, J.D. *Fifty Most Influential Women in American Law.* Los Angeles: Lowell House, 1996.

Foner, Eric and John A. Garraty, eds. *The Reader's Companion to American History.* Boston: Houghton Mifflin Company, 1991.

Read, Phyllis J. and Bernard L. Witlieb. *The Book of Women's Firsts.* New York: Random House, 1992.

Savage, David G. *Turning Right: The Making of the Rehnquist Supreme Court.* New York: John Wiley & Sons, 1992.

Trimble, Marshall. *Arizona: A Cavalcade of History.* Tucson: Treasure Chest Publications, 1989.

INDEX

(Note: Italic page numbers indicate pictures)

Abiquiu, New Mexico, *119,* 120
acting, 56–63, 122–129
Adams, Ansel, 87, 120, 137
Adirondack Mountains, 118
Adolph Zukor's Famous Players
    Company, 127
Africa, 112
African Americans, 2, 24–31
Agricultural Workers Association, 158
Agricultural Workers Organizing
    Committee, 159
Alabama, 140
Alaska, 2, 43, 46
Albuquerque, New Mexico, 91, *91,*119
Alvarado Hotel, 91, *91*
Amarillo, Texas, 116
Amateur Athletic Union, 150
American Academy of Arts and Letters,
    120
American Federation of Labor (AFL),
    160
American Indian Defense Association, 87
American Revolution, 17, 21
Amish, 137
*An American Exodus: A Record of Human
    Erosion,* 135
Anasazi, 96
"Angel of the Cassiars,"
    See Nellie Cashman.
Anthony, Susan B., 18, 20, 36, 77, 78
architecture, 88–97
Arctic Circle, 46
Arizona, 41, 42, 44, 45, 90, 95, 143,
    163–167
Arizona Daily Star, 45
Arizona Republican Party, 165–167
Arizona State Bar, 165
Arizona State Hospital, 165
Arizona's Court of Appeals, 167
Army Air Force, U.S., 143, 144
Army Quartermaster's Corps, U.S., 165
Arrow Maker, The, 86
Art Institute of Chicago, 116
Art Student League, 116
Asia, 112, 120, 137
Associated Press, 150
Astoria, Oregon, 14
Atchison, Topeka, and Santa Fe
    Railway, 90, 91, 93, 94, 96
Atlantic Ocean, 143, 144, 145
Attol Tryst, 63
Austin, Mary Hunter, 4, *80,* 81–87, *83*
Austin, Ruth, 84, 85
Austin, Stafford Wallace, *83,* 83–86
Australia, 142
aviation, 138–145
Aviation Hall of Fame, 145

Babe Didrikson's All-Americans, 150
Baja California, 45
Baltimore, Maryland, 79
Bannock Indians, 49, 52, 53, 54
Bannock War, 53
Baptiste, Jean, 11, 12, 14
Bartlett, Edward, 52
Basil, Andrew, *15*
Basket Woman, The, 85
Beaumont, Texas, 148
Belasco, David, 124
Belloc, Hilaire, 86

Bement, Alon, 116
Bendix Air Race, 139, 141, 142, 143, 144
Bendix, Vincent, 141
Benson, Arizona, 41
Berkeley, California, 137
Beverly Hills, California, 128
Bierce, Ambrose, 85
Biograph Studios, 125–127
Bird Cage Saloon, 44
"Bird Woman,"
    See Sacagawea.
Bird Woman's River, 12
Blackburn College, 82
Boeing, 141
Boston, Massachusetts, 42, 54, 55, 62, 63
Boston Tea Party, 17, 21
Boulder Dam, 87
Bright Angel Lodge, 96
Bright, Betty, 19
Bright, Colonel William H., 19, 20
Bright's Female Suffrage Act, 20
British Air Transport Auxiliary, 144
British Columbia, 43, 47
British Open, 153
British Women's Amateur, 152
Broadway, 62
Bryan, William Jennings, 77
Bureau of Indian Affairs, 52, 53
Bureau of Printing and Engraving, U.S.,
    110
Bush, George, 155

California, 2, 3, 4, 18, 90, 108, 145, 151
    and Dolores Huerta, 159, 161
    and Dorothea Lange, 132–137
    and Lotta Crabtree, 57, 58
    and Mary Austin, 83–86
    and Mary Pickford, 126–129
    and Nellie Cashman, 44, 45
    and Sarah Winnemucca, 50, 51,
    55
California at Berkeley, University of, 135
California Gold Rush, 2, 18, 42, 57
California Mission Revival Style, 91
California School of Design, 90
California State Emergency Relief
    Administration, 135
Calvinism, 34
Cameahwait, 13
Campbell, Governor John, 20, 22
Canada, 42, 43, 124, 143
Cannon, Angus Munn, 66–71, 67
Cannon, Elizabeth Rachel, 69
Cannon, Gwendolyn, 70
Cannon, Martha Hughes, 2, *64,* 65–71,
    68
Canyon Suite, 117
Canyon, Texas, 117
Cape Horn, 58
Capitol, U.S. 23, 112
Captain Gray's Company, 35
Carlinville, Illinois, 82
Carmel, California, 85, 86
Casa Querida, 87
Cashman, Nellie, 2, 40–47, *40, 43*
Casper, Wyoming, 101
Cassiar, British Columbia, 43
Cather, Willa, 86
Catholicism, 6, 7, 85
Catlin, George, *11*

Catt, Carrie Chapman, *111*
Cézanne, Paul, 117
Chaplin, Charlie, 127, 128, 129
Charbonneau, Toussaint, 11–14
Chavez, Cesar, 158, 159, *160, 160,* 161
Chavez, Richard, 161
Cheyenne Society, 100
Cheyenne, Wyoming, 19, 20, 23
Chicago, Illinois, 62, 90, 96, 116, 141
child labor, 102
child welfare, 109
Chilkoot Pass, 45, 46
Church of Jesus Christ of Latter–day
    Saints,
    See Mormons.
Civilian Conservation Corps (CCC), 97
Civil War, 82
Clark, William, 1, 9–15
Cleveland, Ohio, 23, 139, 141, 142
Clinton, William Jefferson, 161
Clipper, 62
Coachella Valley, 141, 143, 144
Cochran, Jacqueline, 4, *138,* 139–145,
    142
Cochran-Odlum Ranch, 143
Coeur d'Alene, 77
Coeur d'Alene River, 74, 75
*The Coeur d'Alenes: A Tale of a Modern
    Inquisition in Idaho,* 77
Coldfoot, Yukon Territory, 46, 47
Colorado River, 87
Colter, Mary Jane, 4, *88,* 89–97
Columbia River, 10, 14
Columbia University, 133
Community Service Organization
    (CSO), 157, 158
Congress, U.S., 22, 103, 104, 107,
    108, 110, 112, 167
Congress of Industrial Organizations
    (CIO), 160
Congress of the International Council
    of Women, 110
Congressional Appropriations
    Committee, 104
"Conquering Woman of the West,"
    See Sacagawea.
Conrad, Joseph, 85
Constitution, U.S., 163
Continental Divide, 13
Convent of Notre Dame, 50
Coolidge, Calvin, 102
Coquette, 128
Corps of Discovery, 1, 10, 12, 13, 15
County Cork, Ireland, 42
Crabtree, Charlotte Mignon,
    See Crabtree, Lotta.
Crabtree, Lotta, 3, *56,* 57–63, *60*
Crabtree, John Ashworth, 58, 59
Crabtree, Mary Ann, 3, 58, 59, 61, 62,
    63
Cronkite, Walter, 143

Daily Colonist, The, 47
Dakota Territory, 10
Dakotas, 14
Dallas, Texas, 148, 150
Darrow, Clarence, 77
Dawson, Yukon Territory, 46
Day, Ada Mae, 164
Day, Harry, 164

Death Valley, 84
Delano, California, 158
Delano Grape Strike, 159, 160
Democratic National Committee, 104
Democratic National Convention, 79
Democrats, 17, 19, 20, 22, 70, 79, 110
    and Nellie Tayloe Ross, 99–104
Deseret Hospital, 66
Deseret News, 70
Deseret, University of, 66
Desert Reclamation Act, 38
DeVoe, Emma Smith, 77–78
Dickens, Charles, 62
Dixon, Maynard, 133, 134
Douglas, 141
Drexel, Katharine, 6, 7
Duniway, Abigail Scott, 4, 10, 32,
    33–39, 36, 39
Duniway, Benjamin, 34, 35, 37, 38
Duniway, Clara, 34, 37, 38

Earhart, Amelia, 143
Earp, Wyatt, 44
Earth Horizon, 87
East Coast, 22, 77, 133
"Eden of the West,"
    See Oregon.
Edmunds-Tucker Act, 68, 69
Edwards Air Force Base, 144
Eisenhower, Dwight D., 104, 143, 153
Eleanor Roosevelt Award for Human
    Rights, 161
El Navajo Hotel, 94
El Paso, Texas, 164
El Tovar Hotel, 92, 96
Emerson, Frank C., 103
Emerson, Ralph Waldo, 82
Employers Casualty Insurance
    Company, 148
Endo, Mitsuye, 7
England, 63, 65, 82, 85, 86, 143, 144
    See also London.
Equal Rights Amendment, 166, 167
Equal Rights Society of Oregon, 35
Esther Morris Tea Party, 17, 21
Europe, 86, 110, 112, 120, 144, 165
European-influenced architecture, 90
Executive Order 9066, 136

Fairbanks, Alaska, 46
Fairbanks, Douglas, 5, 5, 126, 127,
    128, 129
Farm Security Administration (FSA),
    132, 136
Fédération Aéronautique
    Internationale, 145
Ferguson, Miriam, 102
Fernandez, Juan, 156
First African Methodist Episcopal
    Church, 28, 30, 30, 31
Flock, The, 85
Florida, 139, 140
Flyer, Thomas, 79
Flynn, Elizabeth Gurley, 86
Ford, Gerald, 167
Fort Knox, 105
Fort Mandan, 11, 12, 13
Fort Manuel, 14
Fort McDermitt, 52
Fortune Magazine, 137
France, 85
Frankfurt, Germany, 165
Fred Harvey Company, 4, 89–97
Freemasonry, 77
Freemont, Captain John, 50

Gage, E. B., 41
Gallery 291, 116–117
Gallo Strike, 154
Gallup, New Mexico, 94
Galveston, Texas, 153
Gandhi, Mohandas K., 160
Genthe, Arnold, 132–133
Georgia, 112, 140
Germany, 109, 165
Ghost Ranch, 119, 120
Ginsburg, Ruth Bader, 169
Golden Cyclones, 148, 149
Governor's Committee on Marriage and
    Family, 165
Grand Canyon, 90, 92–97, 95, 142
Grand Central Mining Company, 41
Grant, Ulysses S., 52
Grapes of Wrath, 136
Grass Valley, California, 58, 59
Graves Medical Clinic, 71
Great Basin, 50
Great Depression, 7, 147, 150, 156, 164
    and Dorothea Lange, 132, 133,
    135, 136
Great Falls of the Missouri River, 12
Great Potato Famine, 42
Griffith, D. W., 125–126, 127
Groveland, Illinois, 34
Guggenheim Foundation, 137
Gulf of California, 45

Hamilton, Juan, 120, 121
Harquahala Mountains, 45
Harvard, 108
Harvey Houses, 91, 96
Hayes, Rutherford B., 54
Hepburn, Katharine, 153
Hercules Mine, 75
Hermit's Rest, 93
Hidatsa Indians, 10
Hisatsinom,
    See Anasazi.
Hoboken, New Jersey, 132, 133
Holbrook, Arizona, 97
Holliday, Doc, 44
Hollywood, California, 127, 128, 129
Homestead Act, 38
Hopi, 92–93, 95
Hopi House, 92, 92–93
Hopkins, Lewis, 54
House of David, 150
Howard, General O. O., 54
Huerta, Dolores Fernandez, 5, 154,
    155–161, 157
Huerta, Ventura, 158
Hughes, Howard, 143
Hunter, George, 82
Hunter, Jennie, 82
Hurst, Fannie, 86
Hutton Block, 77, 78
Hutton, Levi "Al," 73, 74–75, 76
Hutton, May Arkwright, 2, 72, 73–79, 78

Idaho, 2, 37, 38, 55, 73–77
Idaho Panhandle, 74
Illinois, 4, 18, 81, 82, 90
Imperial Valley, 132, 135
Independence, California, 84, 85
Independent Motion Picture
    Productions, 127
Indian culture, 82
Indian folklore, 84
Indochina, 112
internment camps, 7, 132, 136, 137
    See also Japanese Americans.

Inyo County, California, 84
Ireland, 137
Isidro, 85
isolationism, 109
Italy, 85

Jacqueline Cochran Cosmetic
    Company, 141
James, Henry, 85
James, William, 84
Japan, 4, 107, 112
Japanese Americans, 7, 132, 135, 136,
    137
Jazz Age, 128
Jeannette Rankin Brigade, 112
Jefferson nickel, 104
Jefferson, Thomas, 10
Jemez Mountains, 120
Johnson, Lyndon B., 143
Johnson, Spud, 120

Kaibab Trail, 94
Kansas, 93
Kansas City, Kansas, 93, 96
Kearney Street, 63
Kiki, 128
King, Coretta Scott, 112
Kingman, Arizona, 143
Kingston, New Mexico, 45
Klondike, 45
Korea, 112
Koyukuk country, 46
KUFW Radio Campesina, 161

labor unions, 73, 75, 110, 154–161
Ladies Professional Golfer's Association
    (LPGA), 153
Lafayette, Oregon, 35
La Fonda, 94, 97
Lake Coeur d'Alene, 74
Lake George, 117–118, 120
Land of Journey's Ending, The, 87
Land of Little Rain, The, 85, 86–87
Lange, Dorothea, 7, 130, 131–137
La Porte, California, 59
La Posada, 95, 97
Laramie, Wyoming, 22
Lawrence, D. H., 120
Lazy B Ranch, 163 164, 165, 169
Lemhi Shoshone, 13
    See also Shoshone Indians,
    Sacagawea.
Lewis and Clark Exposition, 10
Lewis, Meriwether, 1, 9, 10, 11, 12, 13
Lewis, Sinclair, 86
Liberty War Bonds, 127
Life, 137
Life Among the Piutes, Their Wrongs and
    Claims, 79
Literary Guild book club, 87
Little Detective, The, 62
Little Nell and the Marchioness, 62
Llandudno, Wales, 65
Lockheed, 141
London, England, 85, 86, 142, 143
    See also England.
London, Jack, 85
Long Island, 140.
    See also New York.
Lookout Studio, 94
Los Angeles, California, 44, 71, 83, 90,
    96, 127, 147, 165
    and Jacqueline Cochran, 139,
    141, 142
Los Angeles Open, 152

Lotta Crabtree Day, 63
Lummis, Charles, 84

Mahoning County, Ohio, 74
Malheur Reservation, 53
Mamizelle Nitouche, 62
Mandan Villages, *11,* 11, 14
Mann, Horace, 54
Mann, Mary, 54
Mansfield, Mike, 113
Maricopa County Board of
    Adjustments and Appeals, 165
Maricopa County Superior Court, 167
Maris, Stella, 128
Market Street, 63
Mason, Bridget Biddy, 2, *24,* 25–31,
    29, 30
Matisse, Henri, 117
McCormack, John, 113
Melbourne, Australia, 141
Mesa Verde National Park, 96
Metropolitan Company, 59, 61
Mexican American, 157–158, 161
Mexico, 2, 45, 120
Michigan, University of, 66
Midnight Sun Mining Company, 46
Migrant Mother, 135, 136
Minitaree tribe, 11
Minnesota, 90
Mint, U.S., 104, 105
Mississippi, 2
Mississippi River, 10
Missoula, Montana, 108
Missouri River, 11, 12, 13
Mojave Desert, 83
Montana, 4, 45, 107–110
Montana, University of, 108
Monterey Peninsula, 85
Montez, Lola, 58
Montgomery, Alabama, 140
Moore, Owen, 127
Mormon Trail, 2
Mormons, 2, 50, 65, 66–71, 137
Morris, Esther Hobart Slack, 3, *16,*
    17–23, *21*
Mother Joseph, 7
"Mother of Women's Suffrage," 23
    See also Esther Hobart Slack
    Morris.
Motion Picture Country Home and
    Hospital, 128
Mounted Police, 45
Muir, John, 82
Museum of Modern Art, 137
Muzette, 62

Natchez, 55
National American Woman Suffrage
    Association, *78,* 108, *111*
National Aeronautic Association, 145
National Aeronautics and Space
    Administration (NASA), 145
National Council for the Prevention of
    War, 110
National Farm Workers Association
    (NFWA), 158, 159, 160, 161
National Historic Landmarks, 90
National Park Service, 94
National Park Service Rustic, 94
National School of Elocution and
    Oratory, 66
National Woman Suffrage Convention,
    23, 37
Nationalist Party, 110
Native American architecture, 90, 92, 96

Native American arts and crafts, 87,
    90, 93, 94, 97
Native Americans, 84, 86, 133
    See also Bannock Indians,
    Bannock War, Hopi, Lemhi-
    Shoshone, Navajo, Nez Percé,
    Paiute, Shoshone, Sioux
Navajo, 91, 94
Nebraska, 101
Nevada, 3, 42–43, 49, 50, 51, 52, 55,
    83
New Jersey, 23, 63, 132, 133
New Mexico, 4, 45, 86, 94, 96, 97,
    115, 120, 156
New Northwest, The, 32, 35, 37
New Oregon Farmer, 35
New York, 7, 65, 86, 125, 150, 159
    and Lotta Crabtree, 58, 62, 63
    and Georgia O'Keeffe, 117–118,
    120
    and Dorothea Lange, 132, 137
    and Jacqueline Cochran, 140, 143
New York School of Philanthropy, 108
New York Times, 47, 109, 137
New York Training School for Teachers,
    132
Nez Percé, 13
Nickerson, Captain Herman, 19
    1975 Agricultural Labor
    Relations Act of California, 161
Nineteenth Amendment, 4, 38
Nipomo, 132
Nixon, Richard, 167
No. 26 Jayne Street, 86
Nolan Creek, 46
Northern Pacific Railroad, 74
Northwest Territory, 37
Nutzhorn, Martin, 132

Oakland Museum of California, 137
O'Connor III, John Jay, 165, *166*
O'Connor, Sandra Day, 7, *162,* 163–169,
    166, 168
Odlum, Floyd, 140, 143
Office of War Information, 136
Ohio, 74
OK Corral, 44
O'Keeffe, Georgia Totto, 4, *114,* 115–121
Olympics, 147, 149, 150
Omaha, Nebraska, 101
Oraibi, 92
Oregon, 4, 18, 33–39, 50, 77
Oregon Donation Land Act of 1850, 34
Oregon State Women's Suffrage
    Association, 38
Oregon Trail, 34, 35
Owens Valley, California, 84, 86

Pacific Northwest, 4, 7, 34, 35, 38, 39,
    73
    See also Oregon, Washington.
Pacific Ocean, 10, 15
Painted Desert, 95
Painted Desert Inn, 97
Paiute, 3, 49–55, 84
Paramount Pictures, 127
Paris, France, 85
Parrish, Sam, 53
Pat and Mike, 153
Paul, James Patton, 66
Peabody, Elizabeth, 54
Pearl Harbor, 4, 7, 107, 112, 132, 136
    See also World War II.
Pedernal Mountain, 120, 121
Pennsylvania, 7

Pennsylvania, University of, 66
Pensacola, Florida, 140
Pet of the Petticoats, 62
Petrified Forest, 95
Phantom Ranch, 94
Philadelphia Centennial Exposition, 37
Phoenix, Arizona, 165
Picacho Peak, 87
Picasso, Pablo, 117
Pickfair, 128, 129
Pickford-Fairbanks Studios, *126*
Pickford, Mary, 5, *5, 122,* 123–129,
    125, 126
Pioche, Nevada, 42–43
Pittsburgh, Pennsylvania, 90
Plains Indians, 90
plural marriage, 67, 68, 69, 70
Pointe Lynde Light, 62
Pollyanna, 128
polygamy, 67, 68, 69, 70
Pomp,
    See Jean Baptiste, Sacagawea.
Port Arthur, Texas, 148
Portland, Oregon, 10, 35, 38
Portland Oregonian, 35
Preemption Act, 38
Prohibition, 102, 108
Prohibition Party, 37
Pueblo-style architecture, 92
Puget Sound, 37
Pyramid Lake, 51, 55

"Queen of the Paiutes,"
    See Sarah Winnemucca.
Queenstown, Ireland, 42

Rabbit Creek, California, 59
Rancho de Taos, 119
Rankin, Jeannette, 4, *106,* 107–113, *111*
Rathborn, Idaho, 74
Reagan, Ronald, 163, 165, 167
Rebecca of Sunnybrook Farm, 123, *125*
Rehnquist, William H., 165, *166,* 167
Reno, Nevada, 51
Republicans, 70, 107, 109, 110
    and Esther Morris, 17, 19, 20
    and Nellie Tayloe Ross, 101,
    103, 104
    and Sandra Day O'Connor, 167,
    168
Rice, Grantland, 150
Ringo, Johnny, 44
Roberts, Reverend John, *15*
Rocky Mountain Revolution, 75, 76, 77
Rocky Mountains, 1, 11, 13, 34, 77
Roe v. Wade, 169
Rogers, Charles "Buddy," 129
Rogers, Ronald, 129
Rogers, Roxanne, 129
Roman Catholic Church, 44, 45
Roosevelt dime, 104
Roosevelt, Eleanor, 104, 144
Roosevelt Flying School, 140
Roosevelt, Franklin D., 104, 136, 144
Roosevelt, Theodore, 77
Ross, Fred, 157, 158
Ross, Nellie Tayloe, 3, *98,* 99–105
Ross, William B., 99, 100, *100*
ruins, 96
Ruth, Babe, 147

Sacagawea, *vi,* 1, *8,* 9–15, *15*
    See also Lisette, Jean Baptiste,
    Toussaint Charbonneau, Basil.
Sacramento, California, 7, 158, 159

Saks Fifth Avenue, 140
Salt Lake Cemetery, 71
Salt Lake City, Utah, 52, 66, 69, 71
Salt Lake County, 70
Salt Lake Herald, 70
Salt Lake Valley, 65, 66, 68
Salvation Army, 165
San Diego, California, 141
San Francisco, 2, 7, 42, 44, 50, 90
    and Lotta Crabtree, 58, 61, 63
    and Mary Austin, 84, 85
    and Dorothea Lange, 133, 136,
      137
    and Dolores Huerta, 155, 156,
      161
San Francisco Panama-Pacific
    Exposition, 63
San Joaquin River, 50, 83
San Joaquin Valley, 156
San Jose, California, 50
San Mateo, California, 165
Sanger, Margaret, 86
Sangre de Cristo Mountains, 86, 87
Santa Clara, California, 85
Santa Fe, New Mexico, 86, 87, 94, 97,
    121
Santa Fe Railway,
    See Atchison, Topeka, and Santa
      Fe Railway.
Santa Monica, California, 129
Schenley Wine Company, 159
Schurz, Charles, 54, 55
Scott, Harvey, 35
Seattle, Washington, 108, 110
Shakers, 137
Shakespeare, William, 128
Shaw, George Bernard, 86
Shoshone Indians (Snake), 1, 9, 10,
    11, 12, 13, 14
Sierra Nevada, 83, 84
Sioux, 90
Sisters of St. Anne, 43, 46, 47
Sky Above Clouds IV, 120
Slack, John, 18
slavery, 2, 25–28, 68
Smith, Alfred E., 104
Smith, Charlotte, 124
Smith, Gladys Louise,
    See Mary Pickford.
Smith, William French, 165
Snake Indians,
    See Shoshone Indians.
Sole Trader Bill, 37
South America, 112, 120
South Pass City, Wyoming Territory,
    18, *19,* 19, 20
South Spring Street, Los Angeles, CA,
    29, *29*
Southwest, *See* Arizona, California,
    Nevada, New Mexico, Texas,
    Utah.
Spanish art, 84
Spanish California mission design, 90
Spanish Mediterranean–style, 95
Spokane Charities Commission, 79
Spokane, Washington, 76, 77
St. Francis Hotel, 155
St. Joseph, Missouri, 101
St. Joseph's Hospital, 47
St. Louis, Missouri, 10
St. Paul, Minnesota, 90, 92
Stanford, Leland, 55
Stanford Law Review, 164
Stanford Law School, 164
Stanford University, 55, 164

Stars at Noon, The, 145
State Department, U.S., 137
State Federation of Women's Clubs, 38
Statuary Hall, 23
steel penny, 104
Steffens, Lincoln, 86
Sterling, George, 85
Steward, Potter, 167
Stickeen River, 44
Stieglitz, Alfred, 116–118, 120
Stockton, California, 156
Suffrage Proclamation, 39
Sullivan, Eugene J., 101
Sun Prairie, Wisconsin, 116
Super Chief, 96
    See also Atchison, Topeka, and
      Santa Fe Railway.
Supreme Court, U.S., 7, 163, 165–169

Taming of the Shrew, The, 128
Taos, New Mexico, 86, 113, 118, 120,
    133
Taos Pueblo, 87
Tarbell, Ida, 86
Taylor, Matt, 59, 61
Taylor, Paul Schuster, 135, 137
Teapot Dome scandal, 101
Tejon, California, 83
Texas, 5, 102, 116, 117
    and Mildred "Babe" Didrikson
      Zaharias, 147, 148, 150, 151, 153
Texas Women's Amatuer
    Championship, 151
Thocmetony,
    See Sarah Winnemucca.
Thoreau, Henry David, 82, 112
Tioga County, New York, 18
Tombstone, Arizona, 41, 44
Toronto, Canada, 124
Tracy, Spencer, 153
Truman, Harry, 104
Tucson, Arizona, 44, 86

Uncle Tom's Cabin, 62
Union Army, 82
Union Pacific Railroad, 22
Union Station, 93, 96
United Artists, *5,* 127, 128, 129
United Farm Workers of America
    (UFW), 7, 155, *157, 160,* 160,
    161
United Nations, 137
United States Golf Association, 152
Utah, 2, 7, 37, 65–71
Utah Board of Health, 70
Utah State Capitol, *71*
Utah State School for Speech and
    Hearing, 70
Utah State Senate, *68,* 70
Utah Territory, 2
Utah, University of, 66

Vancouver, Washington, 7, 54
Victoria, British Columbia, 43
Vietnam War, 112
Virginia, 14, 116
Virginia, University of, 116

Wallace Free Press, 76
Wallace, Idaho, 75, 76
War Relocation Authority, 136
    See also internment camps.
Wardner Junction, Idaho, 74
Washington, 4, 7, 36, 37, 38, 51,
    77–79, 108, 110, 112

Washington and Lee University, 169
Washington, D.C., 23, 70, 102, 109,
    168
    and Dorothea Lange, 132, 135,
      137
    and May Arkwright Hutton,
      77–79
    and Sarah Winnemucca, 53, 54
Washington Equal Suffrage Association,
    78
Washington Political Equality League,
    78, 79
Washington State Federation of
    Women's Clubs, 79
Watchtower, *95,* 96
Wells, H. G., 85
West Coast, 42
West Texas State Normal College, 117
White, Clarence, 133
Whitney Museum, 137
Wilson, Dagmar, 112
Wilson, Woodrow, 79, 109
Winnemucca, Chief, 50, *52,* 52, 53, 55
Winnemucca, Sarah, 3, *48,* 48–55
Winslow, Arizona, 95
Wisconsin, 116
Woman Athlete of the Year, 152
Woman's Christian Temperance Union,
    38
Women for Peace, 79
Women's Air Force Service Pilots
    (WASPs), 144
Women's Exponent, 66
Women's Open, 153
Women's Peace Movement, 110
Women's Strike for Peace, 112
women's suffrage, 4, 86
    and Abigail Duniway, 33–39
    and Esther Morris, 17–23
    and Jeannette Pickering Rankin,
      108, 109
    and Martha Cannon, 67–68, 70
    and May Arkwright Hutton, 73,
      77–79
    and Tayloe Ross, 102, 103
World War I, 4, 79, 86, 94, 109, 117
World War II, 4, 96, 104, 107, 112, 152
    and Dorothea Lange, 132, 136
    and Jacqueline Cochran, 143
Wyoming, 3, 37, 99–105
Wyoming State Capitol, 23, *103*
Wyoming Territorial Legislature, 19,
    22, 23
Wyoming Territory, 17–23

Yakima Reservation, 53, 54
Yarnhill County, Oregon, 35
Yeager, Chuck, 143, 144
Yeats, William Butler, 85
Young, Brigham, 68
    See also Mormons.
Yukon Territory, 42, *43,* 46
Yuma, Arizona, 44

Zaharias, George, *151,* 152
Zaharias, Mildred "Babe" Didrikson, 5,
    146, 147–153, *149, 151*
Zukor, Adolph, 127